A Good Girl's Guide

to Murder

Worry & Anxiety

***

HOW TO HEAL TOXIC THOUGHTS AND BE THE BEST VERSION OF YOURSELF!

Catherine Worren

Table of Contents

1. Toxic Thinking & It's Disastrous Effects

Your mental and emotional state might have an impact on your physical wellbeing. Emotions have a tendency to flow freely and without causing any harm to our health when they are openly experienced and expressed without the attachment or judgment of others. On the other side, repressing emotions (especially those that are associated with fear or are unpleasant) can deplete mental energy, have a detrimental effect on the body, and eventually lead to health issues.

It is essential for us to acknowledge our thoughts and feelings and be conscious of the impact they have, not just on one another, as well as on our bodies, behaviors, and the connections we have with other people.

Negative emotions that are not properly regulated might be harmful to one's health.

Chronic stress can disrupt the body's hormone balance, deplete the brain chemicals necessary for happiness, and weaken the immune system. Negative attitudes and feelings of helplessness and despair can contribute to the development of chronic stress. It's been shown that prolonged stress can shorten our lives. (Recent research has shown that anxiety shortens our telomeres, which are the "end caps" at the end of each strand of DNA in our bodies; this accelerates the aging process.)

Anger (hostility) that is not properly channeled or repressed has been linked to a wide range of adverse health outcomes, including hypertension (high blood pressure), cardiovascular disease (CVD), digestive issues, and infection.

What Exactly Constitutes Toxic Thinking?

We all have negative thoughts from time to time, but dwelling on the negative all the time can be detrimental to your mental wellbeing, leaving you feeling worried and unhappy as a result.

If you're the type of person who takes the time to analyze your thoughts, it can be difficult to tell the difference between negative thinking and the everyday anxieties that everyone has. It is natural to experience feelings of sadness in response to a traumatic occurrence, just as it is natural to experience feelings of anxiety in response to the pressures of one's finances or the challenges of one's relationships on occasion. Problems start to emerge, however, when these emotions are experienced on a regular basis and are widespread throughout one's life (Why I'm So Negative, Angry, and Depressed?).

According to the definition of negative thinking provided by Rethink Mental Illness, negative thinking is a pattern of thinking badly about oneself as well as one's environment. Negative thoughts are something that everyone experiences on occasion; however, negative thinking that has a serious impact on the way you think about yourself and the world and even interferes with your ability to work, study, or function normally in everyday life may be a symptom of a mental illness. Some mental illnesses include depression, anxiety disorders, personality disorders, and schizophrenia.

Just as not everyone who thinks negatively also has a mental illness, the same cannot be said for those who are mentally ill but do not think negatively on a regular basis. When you can't stop thinking negative thoughts, they might have a significant impact on your mental health and quality of life. There are, thankfully, ways to put an end to negative thoughts, but in order to do so, you must first investigate the factors that contribute to their occurrence.

Recognizing Unproductive Thoughts and Behaviours

A cycle of negative thinking is something that can happen to everyone, and according to scientists, there may be a physiological explanation for why this happens. When the amygdala, the region of the brain that is thought to play a significant part in the regulation of feelings, is stimulated, it stays in that state for a considerable amount of time. Concurrently, a recollection of the event begins to solidify in the mind at the same time. The more intense the experience was, the more vivid and long-lasting the memory would be.

Over the course of time, particular recollections grow to be associated with particular feelings. For instance, if you're feeling nervous, it may bring up the memory of getting fired from a job many years ago, and you may continue to have this feeling as a result. When this happens for an extended period of time, it is referred to as "flooding," and it causes every terrible experience you've ever had to rush into your mind all at once.

Negative emotions are like alarm bells, ringing to get our attention and letting us know that something is wrong, therefore it's likely that this process evolved to aid in our survival and get us ready for the worst case scenario. In the meantime, the body releases hormones known as "fight or flight," which cause us to feel tight.

How the Habit of Negative/Toxic Thinking Begins

It's possible that our upbringing is the root cause of why we have a predisposition to have more frequent negative thoughts than other people. There is a vast range of parenting philosophies. In an effort to protect their children from harm, some parents run through all the scenarios that could go wrong and explain them to their kids. Although this strategy might be effective, it carries with it the risk of the youngster acquiring anxiety, becoming pessimistic about life in general, and anticipating the worst possible outcome in any circumstance.

A further contributor is when parents criticize their children an excessive amount, which might result in the development of a pessimistic mental framework. It's possible that you were raised with a big list of things that you "should" and "must" do, making it difficult for you to relax. It is challenging to break free of the routine of daily responsibilities and adopt a fresh perspective when life has become a string of obligations.

Common pitfalls associated with pessimistic thinking:

When you tell yourself not to do something, you are really increasing the likelihood that you will go ahead and do it. It is your parents and instructors that have the "command" voice. Don't forget that you are in command now.

One setback does not prove that you are doomed to repeat the experience or that life is conspiring against you. Avoid making overly broad statements by using terms like "always" and "never."

You might believe that you are to blame, but if you take a step back, you'll probably see that the unfortunate occurrence was not due to anything you did. Consider the circumstances around the event while maintaining composure and focusing on the facts. [1]

Why Do People Have Such a Pessimistic Way of Thinking?

Despite the fact that positive thinking has been shown by scientific research to increase mental wellbeing, reduce stress, and even contribute to improved cardiovascular health, many of us continue to follow thought patterns that are unproductively negative. Let's investigate the impact that negative thinking has on mental wellbeing while also looking into solutions to break the cycle of negativity.

There is a wide variety of reasons for negative thinking. Obsessive-compulsive disorder (OCD), generalized anxiety disorder (GAD), and other mental health conditions may all have the symptom of intrusive unpleasant thoughts. Because negative thinking and depression feed off of one other, both conditions share the symptom of negative thinking as one of their hallmarks. Toxic thinking can be an indicator of mental illness, but it also has the potential to be a natural and healthy part of life. However, negative ideas can have a significant impact on your life, and it is in your best interest to determine the root of these thoughts, no matter what inspired them.

There are three primary reasons that people think unfavorable ideas.

People frequently worry about the future because they do not know what lies ahead of them and they are afraid of the unknown. This frequently results in catastrophizing, which can be defined as the practice of constantly expecting failure and catastrophe. It doesn't matter how you look at it; spending time and effort worrying about the future is a waste of both. Accepting that there is a limit to what you can alter in the future and making an effort to instead focus on the now is the key to letting go of these negative ideas and moving on with your life.

Concerns regarding the here and now It's natural to feel concerned about the here and now. There are a lot of people who worry about what other people think of them, whether or not they are doing a good job at work, and how bad the traffic will be on their way home. People who are prone to negative thinking frequently imagine the worst possible outcome, such as everyone in the office disliking them, their supervisor being about to tell them they've done poor job, and being late to pick up their children because of traffic. Once again, this is because people are afraid of losing control. Although organization and regularity can be helpful in eradicating negative thoughts, you may also find that engaging in some form of practical treatment is necessary.

Have you ever found yourself unable to go asleep because you were preoccupied with something that happened a week ago, or even a year ago? Negative thinkers have a tendency to linger on past mistakes and failures more than others do, while everyone makes and speaks embarrassing mistakes and comments at some point in their lives. Accepting that the event took place and thinking about how you could work to avoid it from happening again in the future is, of course, a more productive way to tackle mistakes that have occurred.

The Detrimental Effects of Unhealthy Thoughts

Things don't always go well in life. However, by having a pessimistic outlook on life, we make it more difficult for ourselves. Let's get one thing straight before I go on to explain how it affects us. If you're going through a difficult period, it's only natural that you'll be thinking back on your past experiences in an effort to derive some kind of understanding and ultimately meaningful lesson from them. That is not the topic that we are discussing at this time. When I talk about choosing a negative perspective over a more positive one, I'm referring to the conditioned behavior and automatic response that comes along with making that decision.

An Optimistic approach is also not the answer to this problem. In point of fact, doing so has no effect whatsoever on solving the problem and, at most, only delays its resolution. For the purposes of this discussion, we are referring to the practice of perpetually viewing the glass as being only half full and focusing solely on locating faults and deficiencies, as opposed to looking for the positive aspects of something or someone. Now, keeping all of that in mind, let's get started.

The effect of having negative thoughts has a wide sphere of influence. There is no aspect of your life in which it is not present. It has an impact on your mental state as well as your emotional and physical well-being. It restricts both your ability to succeed and your freedom to enjoy life.

There are primarily two outcomes that come about as a result of negative thinking in your life:

Your disposition and perspective on life will suffer as a result of this, unfortunately. The simple act of thinking negative ideas can lead to a variety of negative emotions, including sadness, fear, anger, hopelessness, and a general sense of negativity. Your perspective on the world is tainted as a result of these feelings. When you believe that everyone and everything has bad intentions, you will, at best, be cautious and untrusting. You can be hesitant to try something new or say something because you're imagining a bad result, and you might skip prospective opportunities because your negative self-talk is encouraging you not to take advantage of them.

Your ability to accomplish goals will be hampered by thinking negatively. There are always going to be forces pulling you in the direction of your goal and other forces pushing you in the opposite direction. When you have a negative attitude toward the achievement of a goal, it makes it far more difficult for you to achieve that goal. Comparing this to going with the flow of the water, which is smooth and easy, is like wading through muck.

Imagine that you would like to go on vacation to a place that is quite different from where you now are, but also very far away from where you presently are. Your desire to go to various far locations dates back to the beginning of your life. And then you start considering other aspects of the situation.

That once-in-a-lifetime vacation to that faraway exotic location doesn't seem like such a pipe dream any more, does it? When you think in a negative way, achieving your goals will appear more difficult than they actually are. These two adverse impacts have an impact on the whole situation. However, there are further repercussions as a result of this.

It is not good for your health in any way. Negative thinking is a source of unrelenting stress, which in turn creates stress-related symptoms, illness, and conditions, and even disease.

It is detrimental to your sense of self-worth. It is detrimental to one's self-esteem to believe that they are overweight, unfit, unattractive, or unable to perform certain tasks, as well as any other negative label that they have given themselves.
Your self-assurance will suffer as a result. Your self-confidence will suffer if you keep thinking unfavorable thoughts about

yourself. When you have negative views regarding the ability of others, your confidence in their abilities decreases. Your pessimistic way of thinking has an effect not only on you but also on everyone around you.

It causes you to lose energy. Thinking negatively is not only tiring but it uses up your resources.

Moving Forward

Changing your mindset to one that is more optimistic can have a profound impact on your life, but doing so requires some work. Despite this, there are a plethora of advantages, like improved creativity, calmness, patience, and the ability to solve problems. If both parties believe there is a strong probability of a solution and believe the conclusion will be worthwhile, then conflicts will be resolved more quickly, which will likely result in an improvement in the quality of your relationships. [1]

The objective of this book is to shed light on this particular process and to guide you step by step through it in order to accomplish that precise purpose. I have high hopes that you will find this book to be informative and that it will assist you in "Murdering the Toxic Thoughts" and "Becoming the Best Version of Yourself."

2. Know Anxiety & Understand How it Works

Anxiety is a widespread problem that can be just as challenging to comprehend as it is to go through in one's own life. The purpose of this chapter is to provide a framework for understanding what exactly anxiety is and how it manifests itself in people's lives. To be more specific, this chapter will discuss the characteristics that make anxiety stand out as a concept, explain why it is helpful to differentiate it from comparable concepts such as fear and stress, and provide an overview of the clinical classifications of anxiety.

Then, once you have a fundamental understanding of the characteristics of anxiety, we will go over the mechanisms of how it operates. This will include the factors that contribute to its maintenance and perpetuation, as well as the one and only method that is necessary for unlearning any type of anxiety.

What exactly is "anxiety"?
Anxiety and terror are two very similar emotions; how do they differ? What about fretting and feeling anxious? Where does the emotion of being "stressed out" or the tension itself come into play here? What about a feeling of dread? Angst? Panic? Terror? Dread?

Having a clear understanding of what we mean when we refer to anxiety can be one of the most significant challenges associated with overcoming this condition. If we don't have a good understanding of what it is, it will be very difficult for us to determine where it's originating from and what we should do about it. Therefore, to start, let's define our terminology and make it clear what exactly we mean when we talk about anxiety in comparison to other similar notions.

How the Three Stages of Experience Can Help You Define Anxiety

When it comes to discussing anything of a psychological character, including anxiety, it is helpful to differentiate between the three fundamental levels of human experience, which are the physical, the cognitive, and the emotional levels.

- **Physical experiences**

Having a physical experience is the same as having a body sensation, such as feeling hot or cold, tingling or numb, achy or painful, dry or moist, tight or relaxed, etc.

- **Cognitive experiences**

Cognitive experiences can be regarded of as any form of mental or intellectual phenomenon, as well as anything else that is related to thinking. The nature of these interactions is frequently verbal. For instance, the voice that you hear in your head that interprets and narrates the events of your daily life and says things to you like "I just know I'm going to blow this answer," "How could she do that to me!" or "You got this, champ" is an example. But thoughts can also be visual or imaginal, such as the memory of the expression on your father's face when you informed him that you were dropping out of school to go to clown college or the possibility of picturing that you will have a six pack after eight more weeks of green smoothies and spin class.

- **Emotional experiences**

Because they are fundamentally a combination of the physical and the cognitive, emotional experiences are the most elusive of the three types of experiences to pin down. For example, when we are in the throes of rage, not only do we have a lot of thoughts and an inner monologue going through our heads, but we also feel things like heat, tension, or restlessness. In a similar vein, despondency is frequently the result of having unpleasant thoughts or pictures combined with a physical sensation of low energy, exhaustion, sluggishness, or any combination of these. Emotions are the personally experienced feelings that we have after cognitively interpreting something.

Events Vs Actions

Take into consideration the fact that we are capable of having both physical and mental sensations, such as when our stomach starts to rumble and churn or when the notion occurs to us that we should buy bananas when coming back from work. These are instances of happenings. However, we can also directly begin both physical and cognitive events, like as waving to a friend or mentally working through the issue of 14 times 8. These are the steps being taken.

When we have an emotional experience, it is something that happens to us, such as when a loved one dies or when we commit a transgression. They are not activities that we are able to start directly. There is no simple way for us to turn up the volume on our joy or turn the volume down on our rage.

This distinction between occurrences and actions is vital because we can get ourselves into all kinds of psychological difficulties when we erroneously feel that emotions are things that we can do or have direct influence over. It is a fundamental tenet of the vast majority of hypotheses concerning mental health (as well as the fundamentals of neuroscience) that the only way we can directly affect our feelings is by changing our thought patterns, our behaviors, or the settings to which we are exposed.

Let's see if we can place anxiety and some associated concepts within this framework now that we have our three fundamental levels of experience—physical, cognitive, and emotional—and their status as either events or actions. These levels can be categorized as either actions or events.

Anxiety and Associated Ideas

The following is a list of some of the most common terminology associated with anxiety, followed by my interpretation of how these terms differ from one another. These terms are not defined by any official party line, so there is considerable room for debate regarding how they should be understood. However, for the purposes of this chapter, it would be preferable to want to define them right at the beginning in order to introduce some familiarity and potentially some consistency as well.

Factors that Cause Stress

A source of stress is any aspect of our surroundings that can be interpreted as being dangerous or difficult to deal with (e.g. a tiger chasing you or an upcoming exam).

The physiological response of your body to a stressor is what we refer to as stress. The most prominent features of this response are the discharge of adrenaline and the activation of the fight or flight mechanism. Most people feel fast breathing, an increased heart rate and blood pressure, tight muscles (especially in the chest), stomach tightness/butterflies/nausea, dizziness, sweating, feeling lightheaded, and numbness or tingling in extremities like toes, hands, or sometimes the face. All of these feelings are symptoms of your brain's attempt to get you ready to properly manage a threat by either fleeing or fighting.

When we are in a condition of heightened stress for an extended period of time, or when we are in a chronic state of elevated stress, we often use the terms stressed or stressed-out to describe how our bodies feel. It is important to keep in mind that all of these take place on a bodily level, despite the fact that we frequently and incorrectly use the terms "stress" and "stressed-out" to express how one may feel emotionally.

Fear

The human feeling of fear is one that almost always develops as a reaction to some kind of perceptible danger or threat. On the hiking trail in front of us is a dark shape with a curved outline, and as we look at it, we feel panic because we ponder the possibility that it could be a hazardous snake. But as we draw nearer, we see that it's just a broken branch from a tree, and our anxiety begins to dissipate. So we carry on with our hike. Fear is typically experienced in the here and now, has a limited shelf life, and is founded on a rational assessment of potential threats.

Anxiety

Anxiety is a feeling that develops in a person when they have a heightened awareness of a potential risk or danger, much like fear. It's important to note that fear and anxiety are both responses to real threats, but the difference is that fear tends to dissipate fast, while anxiety tends to linger in frequency and severity, even if it's a threat that's merely imagined or hypothetically possible. For instance, after viewing a program about the most poisonous snakes in the world that was shown by National Geographic, we started turning down offers to go hiking because we started to worry that we would come across and be attacked by a poisonous snake. We will soon avoid going to secluded parts of the park, as well as golf courses, lakes, and even zoos. We discover that we have to spend a significant amount of time organizing our days in order to eliminate even the remote risk of coming into contact with a snake.

Panic

A panic attack is an abrupt surge of extreme anxiety that reaches its height after just a few minutes and typically decreases between 10 and 20 minutes after it has begun. Most of the time, panic is caused by an exaggerated view of the symptoms of the fight-or-flight response. For example, "My heart is beating too fast, so I'm going to have a heart attack and die." People who experience recurrent attacks of prolonged panic (also known as panic attacks) are more likely to experience panic when they are worried about experiencing another panic attack. Panic attacks can be thought of as an extreme form of anxiety about anxiety.

Feelings such as fear, dread, anger, and nervousness

All of these feelings can be categorized as forms of fear or worry. Dread, for example, is comparable to anxiety, but it is frequently less specific and more widespread, more strong, albeit possibly not as severe, and significantly more existential in its character.

Worry

Even though we casually use the phrase "worried" to express how we emotionally feel, the best way to think of concern is on the cognitive level. Worry is a sort of problem-solving that has a tendency to be repeated, quick, negative, and self-evaluative, yet it is generally unproductive or useless. Worry is usually often the key reason that maintains stress and anxiety or stimulates it to return regularly. This is because worry keeps us from being able to control our circumstances. It is separate from both problem-solving and planning, despite their similarities.

We hope that this little conversation has helped illustrate how anxiety is related to, but distinct from, a number of different notions that are comparable. The following are two essential takeaways from this conversation:

It is essential that we get as specific as possible when describing how we are feeling. A helpful way to organize this process is to ask the following questions about each particular experience you have: A) Is the experience primarily one of a cognitive, emotional, or bodily nature? both A) Is it something that I am doing (an action) or something that is happening to me (an event)? and B)

As was mentioned before, defining emotions is more difficult due to the fact that they are a mixture of both the bodily and cognitive levels. Emotions, in particular, are the product of a particular interpretation of anything that occurs to us or is seen by us. The term "interpretation" is the key to understanding this situation. Without first engaging in some form of cognitive activity, it is physically impossible to experience any kind of emotion. Even if we cannot change our thoughts, we can influence how we usually think and how we understand ourselves as well as the society, even if these are established cognitive habits. By the way, cognitive therapy and stoicism, its philosophical forerunner, are both built on this principle.

But before we get into ways to change the way we think and overcome our anxiety, let's take a quick look at what anxiety looks like when it reaches a clinical level and transforms into a problem.

Disorders of Anxiety that are Common

When anxiety lasts for a substantial amount of time and causes a significant amount of dysfunction in our daily lives, we can consider it to have reached a clinical level and to be a disorder. To put it another way, anxiety is a condition when it becomes a way of life and has a significant impact on your life. It is important to note, however, that a diagnosis of anxiety should not be made if the symptoms may be more adequately explained by another mental or physical health issue or by the effects of some type of drug, prescription, or other substance. In other words, before you can identify an anxiety condition, you need to rule out other possible causes, such as usage of cocaine, attention deficit hyperactivity disorder (ADHD), and so on.

Listed below, along with a brief explanation of each, are some of the most frequent diagnoses and disorders associated with anxiety.

Generalized Anxiety

Anxiety that does not go away and is characterized by an excessive preoccupation with a number of different concerns (E.g.: failing a test, not being able to sleep, what happens when you die, etc.). People who suffer from generalized anxiety disorder are frequently referred to in the vernacular as "the worried well." People who suffer from generalized anxiety often use the mental activity of worrying as a way to temporarily distract themselves from the feelings that are associated with the things about which they are anxious. This behavior may appear counterintuitive at first glance, but it's actually quite common. Worrying all the time has the unfortunate side effect of raising anxiety and stress all the time (more on this below).

Disorders of Panic

To put it another way, a panic episode is marked by signs of the fight-or-flight reaction, such as perspiration, rapid heartbeat, tightening of the chest, dizziness, and nausea. When a person suffers recurrent panic attacks together with an overwhelming fear of having additional panic attacks or the negative effects of previous ones, they are said to suffer from panic disorder (e.g. going crazy, dying).

Fear of a Particular Thing

Anxiety that is triggered by a certain circumstance or thing, such as fear of heights, snakes, enclosed places, etc. True particular phobias are not as common as you may think. The panic condition that is misdiagnosed as a specific phobia is significantly more common. To put it another way, people have an unreasonable fear that a certain thing or scenario may cause panic, rather than an actual fear that the particular object or situation is harmful in and of itself.

Social Anxiety

Anxiety that occurs in social settings, most frequently when a person is subjected to the observation or judgment of others, is referred to as social anxiety disorder or just social anxiety. It is common for people with social anxiety to worry about how others perceive or evaluate them.

Disorder of Obsessive-Compulsive Behavior (OCD)

Obsessive Compulsive Disorder (OCD) is described as the persistent involvement of either obsessions or compulsions, or both. Obsessions are repeated and intrusive thoughts, visions, or desires that produce a substantial amount of anxiety or suffering in a person (for example, imagining your house exploding because you forgot to turn off the stove). The person with an obsession will try to conceal or ignore these ideas as much as possible. Compulsions are defined as behaviors or rituals that a person engages in repeatedly for the purpose of reducing the anxiety that is caused by an obsession (E.g.: washing your hands seven times before drying them, counting the number of steps in every building you enter, etc.). People with OCD have a tendency to view intrusive mental activity (an event) as if it were something harmful or harmful because they assume that either they are to blame for it or that it indicates anything. This is the core premise behind the disorder (i.e. they treat it as though it is an action).

Post-Traumatic Stress Disorder (PTSD)

When a person experiences an actual or threatened traumatic event (such as rape, murder, etc.), this can result in the development of post-traumatic stress disorder (PTSD), which is characterized by the ongoing experience of the following symptoms:

Memories of the traumatic event that keep popping up and making you uncomfortable.

Avoiding things or situations that are related with the traumatic experience.

Alterations in thinking and feeling that are related with the traumatic event.

After experiencing the traumatic event, the individual may exhibit greater arousal, such as hypervigilance or an enhanced startle response.

One approach to think about post-traumatic stress disorder (PTSD) is as if it were a phobia of recollection. People develop a fear of anything in their surroundings that has the potential to reawaken memories of traumatic experiences, together with the negative thoughts, feelings, and sensations that may have accompanied those memories. As a consequence of this, individuals become fixated on avoiding any form of reminder or stimulus that may bring back traumatic memories. This avoidance can easily lead to feelings of loneliness, sadness, and abuse of substances, in addition to heightened levels of anxiety.

Anxiety caused by being alone

Anxiety that is not age-appropriate regarding a person's separation from an attachment figure, most often a parent, is known as separation anxiety. It most commonly manifests itself in youth (such as exhibiting behaviors associated with school rejection), although it can also happen to adults (e.g. anxiety when a spouse leaves town for business).

How Anxiety Works

We have discussed what anxiety is (and isn't), how it is understood professionally, and the most frequent therapies for it; yet, the question remains as to why any of us experience anxiety in the first place. Why do we allow ourselves to become irrationally terrified of things and why do we allow that fear to persist? To put it another way, how exactly does anxiety manifest itself? And how exactly can we put that information to use for ourselves?

The best thing to do right now is to explain that avoidance is the single most crucial idea in the context of worry. More specifically, we want to avoid our worry in the first place, which is why clinical anxiety persists. At best, the statement appears to be contrary to common sense, and at worst, it may appear to be completely incoherent (Of course, we ought to steer clear of it; it's painful!). So, allow me to explain it in a little more detail. Anxiety disorders are all fundamentally the same at the root of their symptoms. Despite the fact that they may appear and feel completely different, they have the same mechanical dynamics. Anxiety sufferers have learned to fear the thoughts, sensations and emotions connected with their condition. They didn't intend to do this at all; it just happened. In point of fact, the precise thing that individuals do in an effort to alleviate their anxiety—namely, avoid it—is the thing that, counterintuitively, is making it worse. In order to provide an explanation of how everything works, we need to begin with the brain, more specifically with a little cluster of neurons located in the center of the brain that is known as the amygdala. [2]

A User's Guide to Your Amygdala and Its Role in Your Life

The primary function of the amygdala is to protect us against harmful stimuli, particularly those that pose a risk to our physical well-being. Either A) continually scanning the area for suspicious suspects or B) constantly scanning for possibly harmful things. As soon as it detects something that it considers to be a threat, it A) sounds the alert and begins preparing our bodies for combat. This is accomplished by the fact that it causes our bodies to produce more adrenaline and triggers our "fight or flight" reaction. Because of this, our breathing quickens, our heart rate increases, our muscles tense up, and our blood quickly moves from our core and head to our extremities. This allows us to deliver oxygen [3] to our limbs in a manner that is more effective so that we can either fight or run away from the threat. [4]

It's wonderful if you're facing a real danger to your life, such as a thug stabbing you in the alley or a saber-toothed tiger charging at you. In that scenario, you had better cross your fingers and hope that your small amygdala provides you a lot of adrenaline so that you can escape or fight back. When we are faced with a situation that poses a genuine risk to our lives, it stands to reason that the rush of adrenaline and the response that tells us to either fight or flee can be of great assistance.

One of our amygdala's difficulties is that it gets confused between things that are truly harmful and capable of harming us, and things that are just threatening to our survival but don't merit the full-fledged fight or flight response.

How Avoidance Causes Anxiety and Fear Learning

Hiking, in the opinion of the majority of us, is not particularly hazardous. Even while there is always the possibility of being mauled by a wild animal or falling down a cliff on a hike, going for a walk in the woods is generally considered to be a very safe activity.

Many folks, on the other hand, are too antsy to go trekking. They will not accept a hiking invitation from anyone, regardless of who it is from; they will only go for walks along pathways or in locations that they are familiar with; and they will not even watch movies about hiking or going through natural areas. But how is it even possible? Why does uncle Ben not trust me when I assure him that hiking is very safe?

Regardless of what they believe, it's their amygdala's beliefs that matter. And to a significant degree, our amygdalae have a tendency to believe what it is that we train them to believe.

A process known as "Fear Learning" has been initiated in the amygdalas of people with anxiety disorders, teaching them to be overly sensitive to prospective hazards and afraid of things that aren't genuinely dangerous. To further understand this, let's pretend for a moment that you're just a regular person going on a walk in the nearby hills on a warm and sunny spring day.

After being outside for around twenty to thirty minutes, you become aware of something up ahead: a shadowy, winding line on the trail. There is a good chance that your amygdala becomes activated, signaling the possibility of a threat to your safety. (It might be a dangerous snake!) You become aware that your heart is beating a little quicker, and you feel a slight tightening in your muscles. It's possible that your chest is a touch snug. When it comes to dealing with anxiety, the next thing you do is really important.

You have a built-in error correction mechanism in your amygdala, which helps you recognize when something is actually threatening and when it isn't, so that you can either fight or leave in the event of an actual threat. This system monitors how you react to a potential threat and uses your actions to corroborate or disprove the threat's initial evaluation. More specifically, it observes to see if you make an effort to avoid the potentially hazardous thing or if you approach it instead.

You are acting in Fear Learning whenever you avoid the thing that the amygdala has identified as a potential threat, whether you do so by fighting it or running away from it. In essence, you are confirming to your amygdala that the stimulus it identified as potentially harmful is, in fact, a risk to your health and wellbeing as well as your very existence. So that it may Remember it for the next time, and give you a large dose of adrenaline so that you can get away from it more quickly.

Your anxiety will initially decrease if you make the decision to try to escape the potential threat, which in this case would be sprinting away from the dark line back down the trail. This is because the perceived threat is gone when you make this decision. That being said, your amygdala interprets this response to mean the threat it first identified is real and that black curving lines on hiking routes are in fact harmful, as it was trained to believe. As a consequence of this, the levels of long-term anxiety you experience in relation to hiking will actually start to increase now. Amygdala will be more alert to deadly snakes in dark curving lines the next time you go hiking, and will be quicker to activate a fight or flight reaction.

Because even the prospect of going on a hike brings up a lot of worry for you, it won't be long before you scale back the amount of danger you put yourself in on hikes and may even decide to stop going on treks altogether. And every time you limit the kinds of things you can do, you teach your amygdala that something like going hiking is a highly risky activity. You don't realize it at first, but before you know it, you've developed a fear of snakes, hiking, or both, as well as a panic disorder, due to your concern that going trekking would lead to an excessive amount of worry, which, in turn, may result in a heart attack. Yikes!

To summarize, fear learning takes place when, through your actions, you confirm your amygdala's original evaluation of threat by attempting to avoid or get rid of the object that could be hazardous and terrifying. Of course, Fear Learning can be beneficial in a lot of situations. You want your amygdala to remember a threat that is actually present in the environment in which you find yourself. On the other hand, anxiety emerges when the Fear Learning process is applied to items that may look or feel threatening but are not actually dangerous in reality.

Thankfully, the method that the amygdala uses to learn fear can also be used to learn safety, which is the key to reversing any worry which you've built over time.

How to Reduce Anxiety Using Safety Learning

If approach activity (such as talking to someone) is what leads to Safety Learning and a reduction in anxiety, then avoidance conduct (such as running away) is what leads to Fear Learning and subsequent distress.

Back to hiking. When you first look ahead on the route, you notice a shadowy curved line, which causes you to feel a little uneasy. You give some consideration to the possibility that you may just turn around and go in the opposite direction or look for an alternate route. However, at this point all you can do is wait and watch. After twenty seconds, you observe that there has been no movement in the queue, so you walk closer to it. You are experiencing a slightly increased level of fear, but at the same time, you are fascinated about the situation and want to investigate it further.

By now, you've probably noticed that the line appears to be slithering a little, but it's doing so in an unusual manner. It appears like it's swaying. After taking a few more steps, you come to the conclusion that the dark line of shadow is, in fact, the shadow cast by an overhanging tree branch. Not only do you experience an immediate reduction in anxiety, but you've also provided your amygdala with an important education: When out on a hike, you can see something that appears to be a snake from a distance, but it's actually just a shadow. Because of this, your amygdala will be a bit more relaxed the next time you go hiking, and the fight-or-flight response will be a little less likely to be triggered. This implies that you will be better able to have fun and enjoy your trek. This is the Learning about Safety section.

Even though avoiding things that appear or feel dangerous may temporarily alleviate anxiety, the long-term effect is a reinforcement of irrational beliefs that lead to a more constrained (and less enjoyable) life. On the other side, when we take a moment to stop what we're doing and pay attention to our surroundings, we open ourselves up to new opportunities for learning and gaining knowledge. If the amygdala was correct, we can either fight or run. But if we teach it that it was wrong, it gets wiser, and we learn less stressful things, so it's a win-win situation.

Avoidance is a crucial role in long-term anxiety because it incorrectly educates the amygdala to respond to non-dangers as if they really were serious threats, leading to ever-increasing levels of anxiety. It is important for me to emphasize, however, that behavioral avoidance, such as running away from a dark curved line, is not the only way that we can avoid things. In point of fact, cognitive avoidance is responsible for the majority of the time for either maintaining or exacerbating our uneasiness. And concern is by far the most widespread form of cognitive avoidance there is.

But how exactly does one avoid worrying? It almost feels like the opposite—repeatedly playing the terrifying scenario in your head...

The key difference is that we like to think of worry as problem-solving because it provides us the appearance of control and the hope that we can make things better. However, worry actually serves a different goal, which is to divert us from our problems. Our minds are distracted from the feelings of uneasiness, both emotionally and physically, when we worry. Because of this, we are able to sidestep them by focusing on the (seen) problem. Unfortunately, when we ignore sensations of worry, also known as the signs of being forced to choose between fighting and fleeing, we educate our amygdala that these feelings are harmful and a threat to our very life.

This is the conundrum that an anxious person faces: It is difficult enough to be irrationally afraid of situations that are actually harmless; however, to also be irrationally afraid of our own emotions and feelings makes daily life a constant struggle because our thoughts and feelings are always close at hand. It is difficult enough to be irrationally afraid of situations that are actually harmless. Irrational fear of our own sensations is sustained and worsened by the various stealthy avoidance mechanisms we've acquired over the years, including blatant exclusion and behavioral avoidance as well as subtler distraction techniques like concern and "positive self-talk."

Simply ask yourself this one question: What am I teaching my amygdala? If it seems like it might be difficult to identify whether something is genuinely avoidance (and hence making your anxiety worse in the long run), then just ask yourself this one question.

3. Identifying Toxic Anxious Thoughts

When your child was running late to pick you up from the theater, have you ever found yourself worrying that he or she had been involved in a terrible accident? What about the idea that you have the unluckiest possible run of the relationship or life cards when it comes to these areas? How would you like to feel that regardless of how hard you study for the final exam, you would most likely not pass it?

If this is the case, it's possible that you've had some negative thoughts come to you automatically. In point of fact, it is virtually certain that you will have encountered them at some point in your life. The thoughts that come into our heads automatically as a result of a trigger are known as automatic thoughts. They have the ability to make us feel as though we have no control over our own thoughts. They provoke apprehension, guilt, and a variety of other unfavorable feelings in us.

Let's talk about what I mean by "negative automatic thoughts," shall we? Using real-world examples, we'll show you how to recognize automatic ideas for what they are and replace them with more useful ones.

What exactly are these "automatic thoughts"?

As you may have imagined, negative automatic thoughts are the kind of self-talk that rapidly develops in reaction to a given stimulus, before we are even conscious that we are developing a thought. Automatic thoughts are also known as rumination. They are frequently unreasonable and detrimental to the psychological health of us and others around us.

It's possible that the thoughts that run through a person's head on autopilot are different from those of the next person. They are typically connected to the things we've gone through in our lives. In addition, our own anxieties or the messages that we have absorbed throughout the course of our lives. They may concern either ourselves or other people.

Core beliefs are another name for these kinds of messages that are received on the individual level. You might be shocked to learn how similar people's negative automatic thoughts can be, despite the fact that we all have our own unique combination. Core beliefs are another name for these kinds of messages that are received on the individual level. You might be shocked to learn how similar people's negative automatic thoughts can be, despite the fact that we all have our own unique combination.

CBT and autonomic thinking

People whose thoughts get in the way of living can benefit from cognitive behavioral therapy, also known as CBT. This form of psychological counseling is designed to improve patients' mental health and well-being. For instance, when coping with conditions such as depression and social anxiety.

Psychotherapists can assist their patients in recognizing unhealthy thought patterns by employing CBT. This includes any thoughts that come to mind unconsciously. A therapist works with their client to build techniques for confronting their own thoughts and shifting those thoughts into patterns of thinking that are more constructive.

The first step is to increase people's level of consciousness. Their mental health improves as a result of learning how to better regulate the thoughts that plague them.

Users of cognitive behavioral therapy (CBT) don't merely accomplish this during their meetings with therapists. But also by working on self-monitoring worksheets on their own outside of the meetings.

These patients are able to undertake cognitive therapy in their regular life. They develop an ever-increasing dexterity in recognizing individual thought patterns and altering those patterns.

Why thinking negatively is so prevalent in our culture

We all have times when our minds go to the worst-case scenario and we make hasty judgments. We can't help but jump to a negative conclusion, even though rationality tells us there's no evidence that something dreadful has occurred to our child, that we've failed an exam, or that we've had bad luck. This happens even when we can't help but assume the worst case scenario.

Humans have an inherent tendency to look for the bad in each situation since our survival relies on keeping an eye out for dangerous creatures and anticipating potential threats.

Even though we no longer have to worry about whether or not we will survive in the wild, we frequently find ourselves stressed out and unnecessarily nervous about other aspects of life. And if you've ever struggled with mental health issues like depression, stress, or anxiety, you know how challenging it can be to change your negative ideas into ones that are more upbeat and optimistic.

Advantages of recognizing and rerouting involuntary negative thoughts

The fact that automatic thoughts are just that, automatic, makes them a challenge to deal with. Simply bringing attention to these issues and raising awareness can be of great assistance to a great number of people.

The following is a summary of the benefits that can be attained by becoming aware of your automatic thoughts:

Identify the issue

The identification and naming of the issue that is maintaining an unhealthy pattern is the first step toward making changes to that pattern. The issue in question is automatic thought. It might be a huge weight off your shoulders to realize that a negative thought pattern is keeping you down.

When you have identified the issue at hand, it is much simpler to conduct research on the matter and come up with a solution.

Formulate a plan for a remedy

This necessitates establishing a strategy for how we will counteract each unhelpful thought that pops into our heads. Changing this pattern into one that is beneficial and constructive will require the use of the tools that are essential.

Change the way we are feeling

As was discussed before, the domino impact that our thoughts have on our feelings is quite real. If we are able to replace a negative idea with a more positive one, we will have less time to waste on feeling unnecessary bad emotions. It becomes much simpler to face the unpleasant and then to re-channel our feelings into ones that are more beneficial.

Develop a sense of command

You have the ability to take back control of your life and the feelings you experience by reversing the role that your habitual thoughts play in determining how you feel and how you live. Even just having a sense of control over something is already relaxing and relieving in and of itself.

We should not place responsibility on ourselves

Some of our habitual thoughts turn us into our own harshest critics, making us believe that we are to blame for the way that we feel as well as the things that happen to us. It has the potential to wear one out. Life is tough when your own ideas are opposing you.

If we are able to break out of this pattern, we will be able to get a new perspective on the situation. one that can be interpreted in multiple ways by different people. It changes us from a victim or a loser into someone who is deserving of our sympathy, care, and support as a community.

Seek out assistance

Once we have the ability to recognize our behaviors and accept them as "normal," it is much simpler to discuss them with the people we care about. Once we are in this position, we are able to reach out to others for help when necessary, which is highly therapeutic and restorative in and of itself.

Associated Risks of Negative Automatic Thinking

There are a lot of dangers that come along with having negative ideas that come to you automatically. The following are the first five that come to mind:

Unpleasant feelings and experiences

The negative and uncontrollable ideas that run through our heads on autopilot can lead to us feeling uncomfortable feelings. These can include things like melancholy, rage, or even just plain old annoyance. We have no control over negative feelings, but our minds can play tricks on us that make it difficult to wallow in them.

More thoughts that are automatically unfavorable

The more negative thoughts that run through our heads on autopilot, the deeper the hole we dig for ourselves. We are producing an increasing number of them. It can make you feel as like you are being attacked from the inside, which can make it difficult for you to remain objective or sensible. The more vulnerable we are to this downward spiral when confronted with certain triggers, the worse our mental fitness and conditioning.

Victim role

We have a choice between being a victim or a player in the situation.

The expression "things just happen, and there's nothing I can do about it" is at the center of the victim role. And the phrase "I am responsible for how I respond to what happens to me" is the guiding principle for the player role in the game. establishing a certain degree of command over my life.

When we have negative automatic thoughts, we often cast ourselves in the role of the victim. Which could make one feel at ease. The realization that we have no influence over the events that take place relieves some of the stress. However, this approach is extremely restrictive.

Bias toward confirmation

An example of confirmation bias is a tendency to see the world as supporting our preexisting beliefs. When our habitual thoughts are in control of the situation, we search for information that corroborates those thoughts.

For instance, you tell yourself, "I am not worthy," and then spend the rest of the day compiling a list of the instances in which other people have failed to value you. You choose to disregard or minimize the evidence that demonstrates that other people value you. In the end, it turns out to be our reality.

If we don't stop to examine them, our automatic ideas will continue to direct our behavior unknowingly. For instance, because I am a worthless person, I have stopped advocating for myself or caring about how I show myself. Which has the potential to bring about the scenario that we were considering.

A decline in one's psychological health

If we don't make an effort to change our negative, automatic ideas, they can grow to be very powerful. They pose a risk to our mental health because of this, and as a result, they can cause issues such as social anxiety and depression.

Here are three examples of automatic thoughts:

The following are some examples of automatic thinking, which can take many different forms:

I don't think I'll ever find work that satisfies me:

This line of thinking is a perfect illustration of the catastrophic fallacy of automatic thinking. This indicates that we base our decisions on specific pieces of information. And conclude that the worst possible outcome is likely to occur to us as a result.

I have not been a good husband/wife/partner because:

We are engaging in the practice of selective abstraction here, in which we focus our attention on a certain piece of information while ignoring the rest of the information and the context.

In this particular instance, we might be concentrating on a single error that each of us has committed in the capacity of a husband, wife, or partner. Positive characteristics, on the other hand, disprove this instinctive assumption.

It seems as though everyone is out to get me:

This conditioned way of thinking is governed by a concept that we refer to as "generalization." When we make the assumption that we are going to revisit something in a variety of other situations that are not the same as the initial one, this phenomenon occurs. Usually due to one terrible encounter (in this case, being hurt by someone.)

Different kinds of negative thought patterns that are very common:

Thinking that either one is true or false

Having a binary perception of the world around you. There are no gradations of gray. If something isn't up to your standards, you consider it a failure.

Take, for instance, the case in which you have recently begun a new diet and, for the first few days of the diet, you are eating in accordance with the plan. After that, you get a bite-sized piece of apple pie. The whole pie might as well be eaten if I've botched it, because I'm so mad at myself for not being perfect. " What a miserable failure I am!

Overgeneralization

You experience something, and as a result, you come to the conclusion that it "always" occurs in your life. Or you have a desire for something to occur, and when it does not, you convince yourself that it "never" occurs to you. These thoughts are painful because they establish a pattern of failure for oneself.

Take, for instance, the scenario in which you asked someone on a date and they declined your invitation. Your first thought is, there's no way I'll ever find someone interested in going out with me.

Mental Filter

You choose to concentrate all of your attention on one problematic aspect, despite the fact that everything else is going swimmingly.

As an illustration, after giving a workshop, you were given 20 different feedback forms. Nineteen of the forms contained responses that were complimentary of you and the work that you do. On one of the forms, it was said that you could have handled the time more effectively. You only focused on that one "negative" message, while ignoring the numerous compliments and encouraging words others provided.

Negating the Benefits of Something

Because you disregard the good things that have happened to you, you frequently have feelings of inadequacy and un-appreciation.

For instance, while you were performing on stage, you sang well, but you convinced yourself that it wasn't good enough.

Concluding Things Too Quickly

How frequently do you draw a conclusion based solely on an emotion or a concept, even when there is no proof to back up your claim?

An example of mind reading: You appear to know exactly what a person is thinking about. When you observe someone else's behavior or reaction, you frequently jump to the conclusion that they do not like you or that they are upset with you.

Example of a prediction of the future: You have an intuitive understanding that you will have difficulty with whatever it is before you even begin.

Magnification/minimization

Your unique magnifying glass has the ability to amplify a problem, making it appear much more significant than it actually is. Alternately, you have the capability of downplaying both the circumstances and your own redeeming traits.

As an illustration, you made a commitment to pick up some milk on the way back from work. You failed to remember because your head was so full of other things. You have convinced yourself that you are the most forgetful, untrustworthy, and chaotic person in the world.

Reasoning Based on Emotions

Because of this cognitive distortion, it is possible for you to believe that whatever it is that you are feeling must be true.

For instance, you suffer from driving anxiety, and as a result, you've concluded that driving is risky.

Statements containing "should"

You have a distinct concept of how things "should" or "should not" be the way they are. We put the blame on ourselves or on other people when things don't go as planned.

Take this statement as an example: "Instead of listening to you, I should have done it my way." It's all because of you that things didn't go as planned."

Labelling

This misperception is similar to having an all-or-nothing frame of mind. When you do something that you or other people don't like, you give yourself a bad label, and others may do the same. You are completely unaware that your actions do not constitute your identity. In a similar vein, when another person does something that you find offensive or gets it wrong, you are quick to label them and dismiss them as though their action is representative of who they are.

Say, for instance, that you offer someone directions and they end up being incorrect. Instead of admitting that you were wrong and accepting responsibility for your actions, you scold yourself and say things like, "What an idiot!" Or, when someone else disappoints you or makes a mistake, you assign a label to that person, such as "She's a liar!"

Blame and attribution to individuals

You attribute blame or responsibility to yourself for situations or occurrences that are not entirely under your control. The blame game is an example of this type of distortion. When you point the finger at something or someone else, you are avoiding looking at your own role in the problem.

Take, for instance, the scenario in which your kid gets in trouble at school; rather than pondering the events that transpired and the motivations behind them, you condemn yourself as a lousy parent. Or, you may place the blame for your child's difficulties at school on other people, as in the following example: "It's the teacher's fault that my child is in difficulty." She is a horrible role model for the students.

How to recognize thoughts that are occurring automatically

Consider the following example so that we can better understand how to recognize automatic thoughts: Kylie had an extremely hectic day at work, and as a result, when she finally gets home, she feels exhausted and disoriented. Ben, her husband, tells her after some time that he's upset because she didn't see he was feeling sad that day and didn't ask him what was wrong with him. Ben is upset that she didn't notice he was feeling sad and didn't ask him what was wrong.

At this very time, Kylie is experiencing feelings of sadness, frustration, and anxiety because she did not recognize her husband's troubles earlier. She has this thought running through her head, "I am a lousy wife. I don't measure up to his standards of excellence. I'm willing to gamble that he could find more joy with another person. I ought to have paid more attention."

Now that we have that out of the way, let's talk about the measures that Kylie can take to detect her negative thought patterns:

Recognize the uncomfortable sensations you have

Paying attention to our feelings is the first thing we need to do in order to be able to identify when we are engaging in negative automatic thought patterns.

Kylie would be able to describe her feelings of melancholy, angst, and embarrassment. If she becomes aware that she is going through unpleasant feelings, she can use this realization as a key to unlock the thoughts that are responsible for causing her to feel that way.

Determine the idea that led to the development of those sensations

The second stage is to take a step back and ask yourself, "What am I reacting to that is causing these feelings?"

In the example of Kylie, she would realize that her sentiments are the product of her automatic thinking, and she would be able to identify what these thoughts are.

Recognize a pattern

The majority of the time, unhealthy behaviors are the result of automatic thoughts. They are consistent, which helps to bolster the impression that we have. Both of ourselves, as well as our relationships with other people. And the representation of other people that we have in our minds.

It's possible that Kylie is aware of the fact that she frequently engages in these habitual lines of thought whenever she and her husband engage in an argument. Or simply feels as like they've been a party to an unpleasant exchange.

Recognize any cognitive dissonance that might exist

Imagine supposing the exact same event happened to one of your close friends. Would you think the same way about their experience if you were in their shoes?

If you answered "no," then you are demonstrating cognitive dissonance in your response.

Cognitive dissonance occurs when we interpret reality through a lens that is skewed simply due to the fact that it is occurring to us.

Now that we have that out of the way, let's get into a more in-depth look at recognizing negative thought patterns. You can attempt to break away from internalized negative beliefs that often lead to self-destruction by identifying these harmful thought patterns.

Abandonment/Instability

The feeling of insecurity and abandonment that is connected with this thought pattern is brought on by the presumption that an important other person will not be able to provide assistance for the individual. This is a common idea that goes along with the fear that a significant other may leave you for someone else who is considered "better."

Mistrust/Abuse

People who lie, cheat, and take advantage of others will be treated badly. It is believed that this mistreatment is done on purpose in order to cause them harm. It is not uncommon for a person to have the perception that they are being victimized and that others do not have their best interests in mind.

Lack of Emotional Satisfaction

This line of thinking entails the belief that other people will not provide the necessary level of emotional support for the individual. The domains of protection, nurturance, and empathy are the three pillars of support. Nurturance refers to a lack of attention, while empathy refers to a lack of understanding and listening from others (lack of guidance and direction).

Defectiveness/Shame

The person may begin to have the perception that they are undesirable, inferior, or flawed in some way. This way of thinking is based on the premise that if someone were to be "exposed" for who they really are, others would reject them. Because of this, people frequently try to conceal their self-perceived defects by becoming overly sensitive to rejection and criticism.

Social Alienation

The concept of social alienation refers to the perception that a person is cut off from the rest of the world and is unique in comparison to other people. People who think in this way frequently have the impression that they do not belong to any one society or organization.

Dependence/Incompetence

The conviction that an individual cannot manage even the most fundamental of daily activities without significant assistance from other people. This may show as an incapacity to care for oneself without seeking the advice of others first.

Exposure to Risk of Injury or Illness

This refers to the belief that there is no way to avoid or stop something terrible from happening. Some examples of persistent anxieties include concerns about one's health (for instance, a serious sickness), one's emotions (for instance, the sensation that one is "going mad"), or one's environment (for instance, a natural disaster).

Entanglement and an Underdeveloped Self

A person's own sense of identity and growth is sacrificed in order to be so closely connected to another person (such as a parent). This is a common symptom shared by those who feel suffocated, lack direction in their lives, and question their very existence.

Failure

This thought pattern is the sense that you have failed in the past or will fail in the future, as well as the struggle with the notions that you are inadequate and inferior to the achievements of others.

Entitlement/Grandiosity

This way of thinking is characterized by the conviction that one is superior and entitled to unique advantages and rights. A few examples of this would be believing that there are exceptions to rules, trying to impose your point of view on other people, or trying to challenge and control other people without having empathy for their requirements.

Unsatisfactory Levels of Self-Control and Self-Discipline

Self-control and restraint are both lacking in this case. This is especially true when one is fighting an uphill battle against impatience while attempting to accomplish a goal.

Subjugation

This unhealthy way of thinking entails ceding control in order to get the approval of other people. This is done in an attempt to prevent disagreements and separation from the other person. In addition to the belief that your opinions and requirements do not matter and are unimportant, this may also take place. You are attempting to give to others when you abandon your control, but at the same time, you are feeling confined.

Self-Sacrifice

This refers to situations in which a person sacrifices their own goals and needs in order to fulfill the requirements of other people. It's possible that you're doing this because you're trying to make up for being selfish or because you don't want to be the one to hurt anyone's feelings. That person runs the risk of developing feelings of resentment toward other people for the actions that they have done freely if they continue to prioritize the needs of others over their own needs.

Approval-Seeking/Recognition-Seeking

When a person has this belief, they rely on the attention and approval of other people to validate their own worth. The individual frequently ties their sense of self-worth to how other people perceive them and may make an effort to place an excessive amount of emphasis on their status, riches, and power. The goal here is to win people's acceptance rather than simply acquire power on its own.

Negativity/Pessimism

This way of thinking focuses on the unfavorable aspects of life that are observed, while simultaneously making an attempt to avoid or mitigate the positive aspects of life. This way of thinking brings with it the notion that things will invariably go wrong, and as a result, the individual frequently worries about things or complains about them.

Inhibition of Emotional Reactivity

This pattern of behavior occurs when a person suppresses their feelings and their communication with others because they are concerned that they will be treated with hostility and criticism if they express themselves. In order to avoid being vulnerable, the person would frequently repress their anger and sometimes even their delight.

Unyielding Expectations and Hypercritical Thinking

The belief that a person must meet high standards to avoid criticism defines this cognitive pattern. This idea will ultimately lead to pressure being placed on the individual, which will manifest as perfectionism, rigidity, and hypercritical thinking.

Punitiveness

The attitude that other people should be punished for the mistakes they make is known as punitiveness. They may be quick to criticize others and hold themselves to extremely high standards, and when mistakes are made, they may have a difficult time forgiving themselves and others.

How to replace negative thoughts that come to you automatically

Because they originate so deeply within a person, automatic thoughts are notoriously difficult to displace. They have their origin in the fundamental assumptions that we have about ourselves and the world. It is often simpler to consider ways of handling them rather than hoping to just force them out of one's mind with a positive statement. You can start the process of replacing them by doing the following three steps:

Put your opinions up for debate (Socratic dialogue)

In order to accomplish this, it is required for us to inquire about the following things:

Is there any objective evidence to support this viewpoint that I have? What kind of evidence do I have?

The majority of the time, automatic thoughts are founded on one's personal perspective of the world. Not taking into account any objective evidence that may be able to disprove our current line of thought at that time.

Is there a different possibility that I may be considering here?

Because of this, we are better able to generate new ideas and open our conscious minds to the possibility of alternatives that are better for our mental health. It also enlightens us to the fact that the patterns of our automatic cognition are not as set in stone as we had previously believed.

Do I acknowledge the existence of a bias in my thinking?

As was discussed earlier in this piece, automatic thoughts are often influenced by cognitive biases such as overgeneralization or a "black and white" way of thinking. A bias impairs both our ability to judge accurately and our ability to correctly interpret the world around us. When it comes to the state of our mental health, it does not do us any favors.

What possible good can come from thinking this thought?

It is necessary for us to investigate whether or not there is a bright side to thinking in such a manner; if the answer to this question is "no," then we understand that our approach to this issue needs to be revised.

Rather than having the instinctive thought, try having a sensible idea instead.

Simply repeating positive affirmations does not provide much assistance. However, consciously transforming a detrimental idea into a more constructive one might lead to an improvement in one's emotional state. Additionally, it assists you in developing new ways of thinking.

This brand-new idea needs to be:
- Realistic refers to something that is founded on true evidence.

- There should be no space for interpretation, that is the objective.
- Constructive feedback is the kind that pushes us in the right direction rather than the kind that puts us down.

At first, you could find yourself thinking that this method is artificial. However, the more we put in the effort now, the faster and easier it will become in the future. Up until the point where it becomes an unconscious, natural process that is beneficial to our mental wellness.

Take notes and maintain your level of preparation

Keeping a written record of these exercises throughout the process could prove to be very beneficial. To have a better understanding of our mental patterns and how we hold ourselves accountable for changing them.

To properly care for our minds on a daily basis, we need to train ourselves to make this kind of deliberate choice.

When you find yourself going through a rough patch emotionally or carrying a heavy burden, admit it.

In the same way that recognizing ANTs can be powerful, merely stating that you are feeling overwhelmed can also be very effective. Do not immediately adopt a defensive stance and send oneself into a spiral of anxiety when faced with a challenging situation. The first thing to do when you feel mental strain coming on, regardless of whether it's due to stress, anxiety, or another condition, is to accept it.

I know what you're thinking: Why on earth would I ever want to embrace all of the trembling and jitteriness that takes over my head and body? Because accepting it wholeheartedly can require a lot less effort than worrying about it does.

Consider that the fact that you are experiencing this reaction indicates that you are coming into contact with something that is significant to you, and use that information to guide how you respond. The benefit of this is that you won't be obligated to work at maximum efficiency every single moment of every day. That makes my eyes water.

One of the first steps in managing the tension that comes along with anxiety is gaining an understanding of both your anxiety and what it represents. It's possible that you'll find out there's a trigger. You have the ability to take steps to prevent it once you uncover it, or you may discover that you spend less time fearing it.

Devote more time to asking yourself, "Hello, anxiety. What do we need to do today so that we can function together?" and you may find that you are battling against yourself less as you go through the difficult experience.

A friendly reminder that there is always another option, even if it means declining the offer or declining participation. You should ask yourself this question if the source of your worry or tension is a situation: can you get out of it? There is a good chance that you can!

Put yourself to the test by taking baby steps rather than trying to force yourself to think positively

Changing one's state of mind is not as simple as switching from "I feel sad" to "I feel cheerful." To begin, if this were successful, it would make general anxiety much simpler to treat, and it might even be possible to eliminate the condition altogether.

There will be instances when you will not be able to modify your mind pattern no matter how hard you attempt to do so. In situations like these, it is essential to keep in mind that it is sufficient to merely recognize the notion or acknowledge it, as was stated earlier. It's normal to feel down sometimes. It is normal to have worried feelings. Don't push yourself too hard and allow yourself a day off!

When you do have the energy, you may progressively work toward moving past the initial thoughts of "I feel sad" to recognizing there may be a problem and thinking a workaround. You can do this by working toward moving past the initial thoughts of "I feel sad" when you do have the energy.

The more often you bring these ideas to mind, the more likely it is that your thoughts will become less jumbled, allowing you to go to the subsequent level of development and maturity.

Reminder: It is not inappropriate to seek the assistance of a trained professional. If you struggle with anxiety, sadness, or any other mental health condition, trying to trick yourself into having positive thoughts isn't beneficial and doesn't seem true. Seek the advice of a mental health expert if you discover that you are stuck in a thought cycle that you are unable to break out of.

4.   Meet & Greet All Your Feelings

No matter how prepared or unprepared we are to deal with them, our feelings are never far behind, constantly standing by to pay us a visit. You might be surprised to learn how many different emotional states there are, as well as how frequently they occur in our lives. According to the findings of many pieces of research, on a daily basis, we normally experience between 35 and 50 different feelings. As a species, we are capable of a wide range of feelings, from the exciting to the exhausted, and from the aesthetically pleasing to the downright revolting. That's a lot of feelings, and even while dealing with all of them at once can be challenging at times, we shouldn't try to avoid dealing with them. If we make an effort to avoid them or reject the role they play in our lives, we run the risk of missing out on possibilities for personal development and progress.

It is important for me to point out that I used the terms emotions and feelings interchangeably in the previous paragraph because we all do. However, there is a neuroscientific distinction between the two that helps explain what they are doing in our brain and body: Feelings are your conscious experience of the physical reactions that are activated by hormones and neurotransmitters released by your brain, whereas emotions are physical reactions that are activated by hormones and neurotransmitters released by your brain. There is only a slight distinction between the two, but I will elaborate further on that later.

Starting A Conversation About Emotions

You can acquire a better understanding of the range of our feelings by taking a look at the graphic that has been provided for you below. All of them are significant to us, and it is essential for the development of our resiliency in life that we learn how to differentiate between them so that we can both go through them and navigate our way through them. To navigate is to plan, control, and record your progress while traveling; to traverse is to travel across, often under difficult conditions. There is an important distinction between these two terms that I need to point out. To traverse is to travel across, often under difficult conditions. To navigate is to follow a course that has been planned. You ought to make it a point to educate yourself in both of these skills.

Emotions are significantly important for driving the different brainwave states that naturally occur throughout the course of our days and that we are able to navigate. The ability to move in and out of various states indicates that a person's brain is healthy and is functioning well. Brené Brown showed her insights relating to the human experience of feeling vulnerable and courageous. She states in her writing that "We cannot deliberately numb feelings." She is making the major point for actively experiencing varied emotions, regardless of whether you may believe them to be "great" or "terrible." When she says, "When we numb the painful emotions, we also numb the wonderful emotions," she is referring to the fact that we dull both the positive and negative feelings when we numb the painful feelings.

Obviously, you don't want to spend the whole day being angry, terrified, offended, or ashamed of yourself. On the other hand, I would like to issue a challenge to you to think about the fact that you do not want to feel happy, relaxed, excited, calm, or delighted every second of the day either; in point of fact, this can be downright hazardous to your health and safety. I will explain why this is the case and provide you with some methods that will assist you in "feeling all the feels," which will assist you in developing as a person and will make your brain more resilient.

Awareness Is the First Step in Navigating Your Emotional States

Your potential for resilience and self-awareness will increase in direct proportion to the range of emotional expressions that you can express. As the first exercise in this piece, I would want to encourage you to get into the practice of keeping a journal and recording between four and six of the feelings that you experience on a daily basis. You can use the wheel in the previous sentence as a guide, or you can come up with your own names for each of these feeling states. At the same time that you are recognizing those feelings, bring your whole self, including your mind and body, into attunement with them and ask them to describe to you what each of those emotional states appears to be like and how it makes you feel.

Because it makes them feel anxious, a lot of people try to steer clear of challenging feelings. Because I defined emotions as bodily reactions in the previous sentence, you might be startled to learn that any emotion, regardless of whether you believe it to be "good" or "bad," can be stressful. Stress is involved in every single physical reaction. When you laugh so hard that your eyes start to well up with tears and your stomach starts to pain, you may feel compelled to beg whatever or whoever is causing you to laugh so hard to stop. If you want to recover, grow, and get to a place where you can thrive, you need to address some dangerous emotions, and you must do it on purpose. Experiences such as this reveal the stress that your brain is going through even while you are having the "time of your life." Difficult feelings can also create dramatic reactions, but if you want to heal, grow, and get to a place where you can thrive, you need to confront some terrible emotions.

Why Do We Need the Difficult Emotions Just as Much?

The frontal lobe, also known as the prefrontal cortex, is the higher, "thinking" part of our brain. It has been essential to our survival and evolution as a species because it gives us the ability to learn from our mistakes. However, the reactive or troubling emotional responses that often get in the way are a consequence of the frontal lobe not fully participating in the present moment. Your survival-oriented brain is interfacing with your life in ways that are distinct from what your grounded self would choose. To overcome these responses, it is necessary for you to learn how to recognize these interactions.

If the amygdala in your survival brain, which we refer to as "Amy," detects a danger, she begins to manage the data-processing sequence in our brain, and she can begin to shut down your prefrontal cortex. This is due to the fact that Amy, whose primary responsibility it is to ensure that we do not perish, is given the highest priority in the processing sequence in question. She arrives a fraction of a second before the thinking brain has the opportunity to weigh in, determining the level of threat that is being presented.

Simply blink your eyes to illustrate this point

Amy is already analyzing the level of threat to you at a speed that is four times faster than your awareness of that eye blink, and she gets to select how much she is going to include your prefrontal brain in determining how you are going to react to the situation. When Amy's attention is increased by forty percent, the level of activity in our prefrontal brain rises to sixty percent. If Amy's overall health is at 80 percent, her prefrontal cortex may only be functioning at 20 percent. You are currently feeling the influence of Amy taking command if you have ever found yourself later wondering why you had a severe overreaction or emotional outburst in response to something that happened.

Because of this, rather than trying to suppress or suppress them altogether, we need to cultivate a deeper relationship with our feelings. If Amy believes that your well-being is in jeopardy and you continue to reject her warnings, she will yell even more insistently. Because of this, you need to express your gratitude to Amy for keeping you safe while you learned how to make friends with your emotions and for enabling the two of you to grow stronger together.

All of Your Feelings and Thoughts Will Be Accepted

It is crucial to treat all of your feelings as if they are friends because doing so allows you to make the most of the ability you have to rise above challenging sentiments and take control of the process of creating your own experience inside your own reality. It is imperative for us to give any credence to the feelings that our body and mind are currently experiencing in order to improve our ability to use these feelings as directing points of insight for the future.

Let's work together to reframe your experience of intense feelings so that you don't perceive them as obstacles to overcome but rather as openings to gain insight and develop your maturity as a result of their existence.

Building The Language of Our Emotional World

The ability to recognize and accept one's emotions is essential to both resiliency and personal empowerment. It is necessary for those of us who are on a path to healing to consciously confront certain challenging and frightening feelings along the route. Only then will we be able to progress from merely surviving to recuperating, and eventually to thriving. It is healthy to acknowledge and investigate difficult feelings; it is counterproductive to try to suppress or ignore them. When we do this, we impede our natural ability to prevail over them. This is also true when it comes to maintaining emotional equilibrium in day-to-day living. A brain that is properly functioning will constantly engage in processes of self-regulation, shifting us into and out of a variety of states.

When faced with adversity, we as humans are conditioned to disconnect from our feelings in order to cope. Unfortunately, this dulling of our senses makes it more difficult for us to gain insight from our feelings and to allay the anxiety that is building up in the here and now. We are unable to self-soothe and instead go farther away from our true selves when we are unable to be in relationship with our feelings and our bodies. This can lead to an unpleasant cycle of avoidance or even drag us into utilizing toxic substances from the outside world to avoid the data that our emotional brain is screaming at us. Absolutely, screams. Keep in mind that if we consistently neglect our amygdala, she will become more insistent and demanding of our attention. When she begins sending us data, it is because she has reason to believe that our safety is in jeopardy. Let's make friends with our emotions so that we can get stronger as a group.

When we, as human beings, experience fear, our biology compels us to seek out and connect with other people. Because withdrawing from others is not what we are supposed to do when we are scared, our brains are actually more attuned to sensations of apprehension and distress during times like these. And yet, for the time being, staying apart is how we show that we care for one another. Our social isolation is, in point of fact, the product of our social benevolence. However, this does not imply that it is always pleasant to experience. It is important to keep in mind that your emotions are rational, and you should schedule some face-to-face check-ins with the other person within the following few hours or the next day.

The Structure and Function of Emotions

Emotions are often misunderstood and have a reputation for being enigmatic and difficult to understand because of this. Emotions can be useful data for decision-making when they are understood, and they influence nearly every human encounter and choice.

Just like in the movie inside out, our feelings work together like a committee, and they're always at play. The feelings of happiness, sadness, fear, wrath, and disgust are all expertly coordinated by it. We have secondary emotions, which are those that we sense first on the surface (such as wrath and anxiety), and we have main emotions, which are those that are positioned more profoundly within our bodies and our minds (i.e. sadness, fear). Emotions from the outside world serve as a reminder or a signal to us that we need to pay attention to our own feelings. Discovering our internal feelings takes time and patience, but the payoff is invaluable information about how we are truly feeling, what we may be lacking, and how we might respond constructively rather than emotionally to situations. Feelings are not the same thing as facts; rather, feelings merely provide us with information to guide our judgments and actions. When combined with powerful feelings, however, thoughts can have the impression of being facts, despite the fact that they are not facts in and of themselves. A lot of the time, feelings are irrational since they cling to old and new occurrences, thoughts, experiences, and even other sentiments. It only takes about 90 seconds for a feeling to be fully processed if it does not become hooked on something else; nevertheless, this nearly never occurs. Therefore, you should allow the emotion some time to travel through, unhook, and uncover anything more that may be there. A feeling is almost always amplified by surprise, which can make the experience more perplexing or overwhelming. Surprise is a primary emotion. [The emotion of surprise did not make an appearance as one of the basic feelings in the film INSIDE OUT. In my opinion, this is most likely because it would have been too difficult to animate and then choreograph its influence on the other primary emotions.]

Get to Know Your Feelings and Acknowledge Them - Fear

Fear is only fear until we do something about it, at which point it transforms into anxiety or worry. Anxiety and worry are both forms of fear. When we allow ourselves to fully experience our fears, that fear can transform into excitement. There are moments when we push ourselves further into things that make us nervous and into new challenges. When we allow ourselves to feel all of our emotions (physical and emotional safety in mind), we can feel energized and alive. The practice of exposing oneself to their fears in a controlled setting while maintaining a level of composure is called exposure therapy. When you are feeling terrified in a new relationship or when you are going through an emotionally challenging moment with a loved one, try leaning toward your fear. You can meditate or practice relaxation while keeping your specific phobia in mind. The next step is to reflect on what transpires as a result of that encounter; how did you feel? What did you learn?

Shame

Meet **Shame**, also known as Guilt, Embarrassment, and Humiliation. Brene Brown describes Shame as the experience of having a negative opinion of oneself. When we do something wrong and then feel horrible about it, we experience guilt. We experience embarrassment when we feel horrible about something that happened to us and when we feel alone in it at the same time. When we experience humiliation, it's because we feel horrible about ourselves because of something that happened to us that we didn't deserve. In a nutshell, all of these sensations originate from the experience of feeling awful, and then we do something about that. We create or give meaning to this "poor feeling." Feeling guilty may have a purpose, as it may enable us to correct something that we've done incorrectly. It's possible that experiencing shame can help us realize that we require consolation regarding a traumatic occurrence that other people have also been through. The experience of humiliation may give us the opportunity to extend compassion or kindness to oneself that other people either did not provide or failed to provide in some way. If any of these sentiments continue for an excessively long period of time, then they lose their positive function, which is connection. The result of this is that we come to believe that we are "evil" people who are unworthy of being loved. We have the feeling that we are "not good enough." Practice: Reflect on the aspects of your life in which you do not feel "good enough." What kind of a tale are you spinning for yourself? Are we dealing with facts or feelings here? What feelings have become stale and ingrained? What are the emotions that require care and comfort? To rewrite your story, you need to give yourself permission to do so. You may try writing it from the point of view of a buddy who is empathetic. After that, you should read it out loud to a loved one or a reliable friend. According to Brene Brown, the most effective treatment for shame is to talk about it with other people and to feel connected to them through the emotional anguish that you are experiencing.

Anger

The combination of **Anger** and hurt is what gives rise to the emotion known as hatred; the opposite of hate is passion, which also incorporates feelings of fury and hurt. Similar to worry, anger is a feeling that serves as a signal. It serves as a signal to us that we are experiencing a feeling or having an encounter that requires either our protection or our attention. When we push away our feelings of anger, we open ourselves up to the possibility of experiencing resentment, which is the emotion we feel when we desire something but do not get it. When not addressed, our ire has the potential to develop into outrage. Irritation is frequently the first emotion we feel when we begin to exhibit signs of anger or anxiety. Our tendency to bottle up our rage might lead to a sensation of numbness. Taking revenge is justifying the actions we take out of anger. To summarize: anger plus action plus lack of attention equals additional anger and misery. Putting this into practice can help you recognize your own and others' furious reactions as signs of anguish. These signs constitute a request for reassurance, connection, and love. Consider very carefully what you believe you may need in order to properly give love to either yourself or the person you love who is furious. It's possible that showing love means protecting someone and keeping yourself safe until the situation is less volatile and you can engage with them. It's also possible to show love by showing compassion and understanding to oneself, as well as making time for the healing process.

Sadness

Meet **Sadness** (Grief, Depression): Sadness presents itself as anger when we allow our desire for emotional attention and connection to go unsatisfied. Grief and depression are also forms of sadness. One of the most authentic and unadulterated feelings that we are capable of having is sadness. When we allow ourselves to feel complete sadness, we are able to let go of that emotion. Despite this, we frequently prevent ourselves from experiencing feelings of grief in an effort to avoid experiencing emotional discomfort. Grief is characterized by feelings of sadness brought on by the absence of, or the loss of, someone or something significant to the sufferer. The pain of loss can be lessened over time and our hearts can heal if we talk about it. When it is repressed or ignored, grief can lead to feelings of alienation and loneliness, along with a host of other negative outcomes associated with pain, such as addiction, abuse, and extramarital affairs. A prolonged and repressed feeling of sadness characterizes depression. Problems in a person's life condition, their biology, their past, and/or the interactions they have with others can all contribute to the development of depression. For the symptoms of depression to be alleviated, in-depth healing and treatment are required. Honoring feelings of melancholy when they arise is a good practice. Sadness teaches us that we love and that we can be loved by others. When we feel sad, it's a sign that we need to connect with other people. It serves as a constant reminder that we are alive, feeling beings. When we open the door to the experience of grief and let it come and go freely in our life, we might start to recognize that joy frequently follows in its wake.

Joy

Meet **Joy**: Joy is a continuous sense of happiness that can occur at various times and places throughout our life. We make the mistake of thinking that it is a permanent condition of being. The emotion of happiness is one that might be ephemeral and it is healthy for it to come and go throughout one's life. Happiness is not something that we acquire; rather, each instant presents us with the opportunity to experience it or not. Do you recall what the character of JOY discovered in the movie Inside Out when she saw Riley crying after she had a bad game of hockey? JOY discovered that crying (or expressing sadness in any other way) is a signal to others that we require comfort from them. When we find joy in our life on a consistent basis, we have the ability to experience contentment. When there is a surplus of joyous energy within us, we experience ecstasy. If we let our happiness run wild and let it disturb our connections to others and to ourselves, we run the risk of developing manic symptoms.

5. Manage Emotions

Emotions are quite potent. Your disposition influences the way you communicate with other people, how much money you spend, how you respond to difficult situations, and how you spend your time.

Acquiring mastery of one's feelings can contribute to the development of one's mental fortitude. To our great relief, the ability to better control one's feelings is something that can be developed by everybody. Managing your emotions is a skill, and like any other skill, it involves practice and commitment on your part.

It's possible that you're underestimating the significance of your capacity to feel and communicate your emotions. Emotions, which are experienced responses to certain circumstances, are a significant factor in your responses. It's possible to have access to vital information about decision-making, interpersonal relationships, daily interactions, and self-care when you're in tune with your instincts.

Even though your feelings can play a beneficial part in your day-to-day life, when they begin to feel out of control, they can take a toll on both your mental health and the quality of your interactions with other people.

Any emotion, including elation, delight, and others that you may ordinarily consider to be positive, is capable of intensifying to the point where it is impossible to maintain control over it. You may, however, reclaim control of the situation with some effort and practice. According to the findings of two separate research conducted in 2010, having effective emotional regulation abilities may be associated with higher levels of wellbeing. In addition, the second study discovered a possible connection between these skills and monetary success; hence, putting in some effort in this area may literally pay off in the long run.

The Importance of Being Able to Manage Your Emotions

Have you ever had one of those days where it seems like everything that may go wrong, does? When it seems as though all of your plans have fallen apart and the whole world is working against you, how can you keep going? Perhaps this is the case. It's possible that the sensation of having your efforts undermined by the outside world is simply your brain's method of letting you know that you need to make some adjustments. This uneasy feeling, on the other hand, has the potential to develop into more significant issues if we fail to pay attention.

It is common knowledge that our feelings can have a significant influence on the course of our lives. The quality of life that we experience is impacted not just by how we feel and behave, but also by our emotional condition. People who are joyful, as an illustration, have a greater propensity to be in better physical condition than those who are nervous or depressed. There are a lot of people who are questioning why it's so necessary to regulate our emotions and why we need to make time for it, and this chapter will provide some answers to these questions.

To begin, let's investigate the ways in which our minds and body interact, from head to toe. In addition to this, we are going to compare and contrast what occurs to us emotionally and physiologically when we are furious versus when we are sad. In the final part of this series, we will talk about what it's like when our feelings are out of control and how to stop thinking that life is out to get us.

The significance of one's feelings

Emotions have the potential to exert a significant influence on our lives. Our mental health determines not only how we feel but also how we behave and the overall quality of life that we have. People who are joyful, as an illustration, have a greater propensity to be in better physical condition than those who are nervous or depressed.

It is impossible to overstate the significance of one's feelings. They are the foundation upon which our lives are built. Your mood and quality of life are both affected when you aren't in a good mood. You may also be feeling negative and unmotivated. Because of this, it is essential to make an effort to keep one's emotions under control in order to make progress toward one's goals in life.

There are many strategies that will be of assistance to you in this endeavor. For instance, when you feel a strong negative emotion coming on, try thinking about something positive, such as your favorite place or moment, and then imagine how you will feel after you have achieved your goal. There are many strategies that will be of assistance to you in this endeavor. This may at first appear to be ridiculous, yet it is effective!

How our mental states influence our bodies

Agitation is a condition of mental agitation that is characterized by a strong desire to move around or behave in an uncontrolled manner. Our unfavorable feelings trigger physiological responses in our bodies, some of which might be detrimental to our health. These responses have the potential to have an impact, not just on our internal mental state, but also on how others perceive us. This chapter is going to explore some of the bodily reactions that occur when we experience negative emotions, as well as ways to control those reactions so that they do not have a harmful impact on our bodies.

The way in which our bodies react physically to the feelings we experience is something that we acquire accustomed to as we develop into humans. I am certain that the vast majority of you have known what it is like to feel fear, anger, or sadness at some point in your lives and to have a specific bodily reaction to those emotions, such as a faster heart rate, sweaty palms, or a tightness in the chest or shoulders (for example). Our bodies are predisposed to react in particular ways, which have evolved over millennia to ensure our survival. We can benefit from short bursts of negative emotions like anger or fear or sadness, but if these reactions remain over an extended length of time, our health can suffer. Some typical physiological responses include chest tightness, dizziness, and shallow breathing. a rapid heartbeat in addition to palpitations, Alterations in blood pressure, stress on the muscles, and other symptoms shaking their hands and/or feet, perspiring, and/or both Sensing themselves to be "keyed up" and tense, sentiments of hopelessness or fear that are difficult to control, ideas that are detrimental to oneself, or both.

When we are experiencing sentiments of intense positive emotions, we also have the ability to have physical reactions.

These pleasant states of mind are frequently accompanied by a surge of euphoria, a quickening of the pulse rate, the relaxing of the muscles, and a feeling of warmth.

When we are able to recognize and take control of our feelings, we are able to exert control over both the mental and physical aspects of how we experience life. In order to accomplish this, we need to have a solid understanding of these physical reactions, which will allow us to exert a greater degree of control over them.

Angry VS Sad- What Happens, and Why It Matters

A decrease in physical arousal is something that happens to us when we feel sad. This may involve feeling more peaceful and quiet than usual, as well as having less energy than usual. The question of whether or not it is possible to entirely suppress your feelings is still open for discussion; however, it is generally accepted that the physiological responses become far less severe when one is experiencing sadness. It's possible that this also has something to do with the fact that there isn't a fear reaction that indicates danger, which is something that would normally be linked with anger or worry. These responses are triggered within our bodies by the neurological system as a means of assisting us in dealing with the effects of stress as well as any other event that may pose a risk to our safety.

On the other hand, when we feel furious, we experience an increase in physical arousal, which manifests itself in a number of different ways, including a faster heart rate and breathing rate, tense muscles, a flushed face, and sweaty palms.

Sadness is typically accompanied by thoughts and emotions such as loss and helplessness. Because there is little to no threat most of the time, our bodies have been trained to relax (except in cases where sadness arises from grief). However, the emotion that arises from anger may be a component of a response to defend oneself from harm. When we sense fear, our bodies react in a similar manner. Because of this rise in arousal, we are better equipped to deal with the potential physical dangers that come along with being furious. Frustration and disappointment are two emotions that can contribute to sentiments of anger. These emotions can be accompanied by unfavorable thoughts about oneself or others. Although this may not be harmful to our bodies in and of itself, it can have a significant impact on how we think of ourselves and how we behave toward other people.

How to Keep Our Feelings in Check and Stop Thinking That Life Is Trying to Screw Us Over

There are a variety of strategies available to assist you in regaining control of your feelings and dispelling the notion that life is conspiring against you. Keeping a journal is one method that can be utilized. When we aren't sure why we're experiencing a certain emotion, it might be helpful to keep a journal so that we can reflect on the events of the previous day or week and try to piece together why we're feeling the way we are. Sometimes it's difficult to understand why we're feeling a certain way. Meditation with an awareness of the present moment is another method. It is common for people to experience a sensation of disconnection from their surroundings and their senses when they are under emotional or mental strain. Your mind can be cleared, your worry can be quelled, and you can experience a sense of tranquility that can linger for days with only a few minutes of mindfulness meditation.

You can also learn how to "ride the wave" of emotions such as anger, anxiety, or sadness. This is something you can do if you want to do something else. It is perfectly normal to experience powerful and unexpected emotions; this is especially true when one is feeling frustrated. Try to picture these emotions as waves crashing on the shore rather than allowing yourself to be swept away by them. A wave is nothing more than an emotion that travels through your body and eventually comes to an end, just like any other wave on the ocean

To begin implementing this strategy, simply take a few long, slow breaths. You can relax your neural system, which is what causes all of these physical sensations that we can interpret as bad emotions, by practicing deep breathing. Your nervous system is what causes these symptoms. After that, all you need to do is go back to how you felt when you had to cope with waves in the past.

Next, envision a wave that you have experienced in the past, and attempt to recall what the circumstances were at the time. Put your hands over your eyes and try to conjure up the sensation of being hit by that wave for the first time, as well as the sensation of it washing away from you now.

Understanding that coping with unexpected surges of emotion is totally normal and something that everyone goes through at some point in their lives can be of assistance to you in coming to terms with this reality. Our neurological systems become less active as these feelings move through us, much in the way the ocean becomes less agitated after a wave has passed a shore.

The advice that we have covered in this chapter is merely the tip of the iceberg in terms of what is available. There is a wide variety of additional strategies that might be of use to us in dealing with our thoughts and feelings. It is important to keep in mind that the waves that are hitting you will eventually recede. Always make an effort to take a few slow, deep breaths before approaching them, and keep in mind all of the positive outcomes that will result from doing so.

Emotions are something that we all feel, perhaps some more than others. There are some people who are able to keep their sentiments under check, while for others this can be a difficult task. To have a healthy and happy life in this world, it is essential to have a working knowledge of how our brains operate and to respond appropriately. For instance, if we are aware that different emotions have distinct physiological effects on the body, then we won't necessarily have the impression that the world is conspiring against us when we experience negative emotions in the here and now.

Recognize & accept your feelings

The process of being able to identify and accept one's own feelings is referred to as emotional awareness. Being emotionally self-aware can provide you with the tools necessary to effectively manage and improve your mental hygiene. When people experience a particular feeling, there is frequently a corresponding mental or physical reaction that goes along with it. It is possible to determine when you are feeling a certain emotion by paying attention to the mental and bodily signs that arise within you at that time.

Take for instance the fact that you are currently seated in a restaurant. You will have lunch with a friend who is coming to meet you. Already she is ten minutes behind schedule. The thought crosses your mind, "Geez, she always keeps me waiting." And you become acutely aware of the fact that you are rhythmically tapping your straw against your water glass. You become aware of the fact that you are experiencing impatience as a consequence of both the idea and the action that follows. [4]

Observe your behaviors and thoughts for at least a day, preferably two. How do they provide you any indication as to the state of your emotions? As a first step toward developing more emotional awareness, keep a notebook in which you record these observations.

Why it's vital to recognize and accept your feelings

One of the most valuable talents you can acquire is self-awareness, as well as the ability to control your feelings and behaviors in response to them. People who are adept at monitoring how they feel and who are able to calm themselves down or alter their behavior are really more likely to succeed in life, have healthy relationships, and manage challenges and setbacks more effectively.

The intensity of one's feelings can at times be too much for one to bear. Adults and children alike may have difficulty managing their responses to their feelings, resulting in behaviors that appear to be mostly out of their control. This challenge can cause both groups to act in ways that are counterproductive. Have you ever been so angry that you accidentally hurt the feelings of someone you love by saying something they didn't deserve? Then, when you had some time to collect your thoughts, you came to the conclusion that you had let your feelings get the best of you, and you wished you had handled the situation differently.

We have all been guilty of this behavior at one time or another, but as children mature, it is imperative that they learn how to exercise self-control over their feelings and improve their ability to respond appropriately to challenging circumstances.

Acquiring an understanding of the rationale underlying your feelings

It is via our emotions that we may form relationships with the people in our lives and learn what makes us happy and what doesn't.

Our feelings are similar to an internal compass in that they assist us in determining how a certain circumstance makes us feel. As a result, we may make better decisions about whether or not we want to be in that scenario and better understand our priorities.

We need to be able to identify when we are feeling a certain emotion, understand what that emotion is, and comprehend what it is attempting to convey to us. For example, if a child spends time with a group of people that make them feel bad about themselves, worried, and under pressure, it is critical that they identify this and understand that their feelings are telling them that this isn't the best scenario for them.

As long as they can pay attention and respond appropriately, they will be attracted to those who help them improve their self-esteem.

Experiencing a greater sense of mastery of Emotions

Our states of mind and conduct can be profoundly influenced by our emotions. Friendships, family connections, academic performance, and our overall feelings of enjoyment can all be negatively impacted when we are frequently experiencing negative emotions such as anger, anxiety, or worry.

When children have a lot of negative feelings, it's common for them to feel that they don't want to participate in extracurricular activities or interests outside of school. It is crucial that we help ourselves, our loved ones, and our children understand when they are feeling miserable in order for them to determine why they are feeling this way and attempt to find a solution that would make them feel better about themselves. It will have a significant impact on their sense of purpose and their sense of ownership of their life if they are able to get the abilities to reflect on their feelings and recognize that they are in control of how they feel.

Unpleasant feelings are often accompanied by negative ideas

It is possible that we will think unhappily as a result of our inability to notice when we are experiencing unhappiness. It is of the utmost importance that we make it clear to youngsters that they are the ones in charge of the thoughts that go through their heads. If they spend a lot of time thinking negative thoughts about themselves, such as "I am not good enough" or "No one likes me," then this is going to have an effect on their frame of mind as well as the way they evaluate the circumstances in which they find themselves.

Teaching youngsters that they have the ability to modify their ideas and decide what they think can alter their perceptions and help shape them into young people who can reframe negativity, be happier, and have faith in their own capabilities.

The takeaway from this that you and your loved ones need to understand is that if someone believes they can accomplish something, then in all likelihood they will be able to do so. The only thing required of them is to have faith in it. Noticing when we are feeling uncomfortable and actively working to change our negative thoughts is the first step in improving our mental health and overall wellness.

It indicates that we are able to seek assistance

When we are going through tough circumstances, we may require assistance from those closest to us, such as our parents or other caregivers, our teachers, or a close friend. It is crucial to be able to understand when you need help dealing with your emotions, but children frequently are unable to figure this out on their own. They require continuous guidance and support with their feelings in order to learn how to regulate their anxiety and stress levels.

When they are experiencing sentiments that are too much for them to handle, often times all that a youngster needs is a hug from a trusted adult. Or someone who will listen to them without passing judgment, with the emphasis being placed on how they are feeling rather than the circumstances. Our younger children and adolescents need to be made aware of the fact that they can discuss their significant emotions with a trusted adult who will assist them in navigating those emotions.

Children can develop healthy ways to manage their emotions by first learning how to communicate with the people around them and then figuring out what those people need from them in order to receive assistance.

It makes you a more reliable and trustworthy buddy

When you have the ability to identify your own feelings, take control of them, and convey them to other people, you will be in a position to assist other people in developing these skills as well. Teens and youngsters who are able to get particularly excellent at understanding people's feelings will be able to identify when the people around them are not feeling very pleased and will be able to respond correctly and support those around them.

As they get older, the fact that they will be able to support their siblings, friends, and other people in their environment will assist them in developing better relationships.

Give yourself permission to experience all of your feelings

When someone is unhappy, angry, anxious, ashamed, or in any other kind of discomfort, they frequently engage in activities in the hope that they will feel better. It's vital to let yourself feel your emotions as they come up rather than trying to change them, even if this may be a normal reaction for you to have in this situation. Spend some time reflecting on your sentiments and giving yourself permission to simply be with them. It is a necessary stage in the process of overcoming them, despite the fact that it may be unpleasant. [5]

Don't pass judgment on either yourself or your feelings. Simply allow yourself to experience them and accept them so that you may go on.

This does not imply that you should wallow in rage or misery for an extended period of time after the event. Seek the assistance of a therapist if you are experiencing these feelings and find that you are unable to let go of your emotions or work through them on your own.

Communicate your feelings in a constructive manner

After you have gained the ability to recognize the mental and physical clues of your emotions, the next step is to discover healthy ways to express those emotions. Expression of feelings is important since bottling up or repressing them can result in negative health outcomes such as depression or anxiety. There are various constructive and beneficial methods that you can communicate your emotions, including the following: [6]

One of the most effective ways to let your emotions out is to discuss them with other people. [7] Just make sure that the person with whom you are sharing is someone who is supportive and does not pass judgment. Think about talking to your closest friend, a sibling, or a professional counselor.

Writing out your thoughts and emotions can also be therapeutic. Keep a journal in which you record your thoughts. You can take a look at these entries at a later time to determine if there are any recurring themes. Writing in a journal can be beneficial to one's mental health in general, but it is especially beneficial when the journal is utilized not only for expressing emotions but also for finding solutions to problems.

If you need to, you should cry. People may suppress their feelings of sadness out of guilt or shame, even when they are experiencing such feelings. At other times, you may experience feelings of melancholy but find that you are unable to cry. You can assist yourself shed those tears by watching a movie, reading some literature, or listening to some music that speaks to your emotional state.

Relax and let go of the strain. Because the things you say and do when you're furious might not be socially appropriate, expressing anger can be one of the more challenging feelings to communicate. For instance, it is probably not a good idea to yell at the people you care about, smash items, or pound walls when you are angry. Instead, you can try using some of the same tactics that you use to manage your stress in order to master your anger. You could find that doing a strenuous workout or yelling into a pillow helps.

Take care with the way that you communicate your feelings to other people. When you are having a conversation with someone and you become upset, it is best to take a break and then return to the topic when you are in a better position to communicate how you feel. When you want to avoid making charges but still take responsibility of your anger or other sentiments, use "I feel" words. For example, rather than saying, "You make me so angry," you could say, "When you speak to me in that manner, I feel hurt and angry." You're such a jerk!"

Realize that both good and negative feelings are necessary for healthy functioning

Joy, enthusiasm, and love are all emotions that humans like expressing. However, it could appear to be the best course of action to push away unwanted emotions. You may have been brought up with the belief that displaying negative emotions such as wrath, humiliation, or frustration was unacceptable, and as a result, you suppress these feelings. Keeping your feelings bottled up won't make them go away; in fact, it's possible that doing so will make them even more intense. Emotional repression can be a factor in the development of mental health problems such as anxiety and depression. [8]

Despite how tempting it may seem, you must fight the urge to bury or suppress your negative emotions. Negative emotions such as rage or despair are just as vital to your mental health as positive feelings are. These emotions provide you with information about the things that are important to you as well as the aspects of yourself or your surroundings that may need to be altered. [9]

Methods for Taking Control of Your Emotions

It's natural for people to struggle at times to maintain control over their feelings and behaviors; it's just a part of being human. However, if it happens frequently, the regulatory measures could be helpful. You're just going about your day like any other when suddenly everything changes. Suddenly, you find that you are helpless, anxious, or otherwise unable to manage your feelings.

You've probably heard some common pieces of advice for helping yourself, such as "stop what you're doing and take a deep breath," as well as some less useful pieces of advice, such as "simply control yourself." However, despite being in the passenger seat, you can't help but have the impression that your feelings are in control of the situation.

When something like this occurs, it can be helpful to remind yourself that your sentiments exist for a purpose. There is no such thing as a "bad" feeling because there are no such things. Make an effort, if at all possible, to find thankfulness for your feelings because they carry information that is valuable to you. If at all possible, you should make an effort to accept feelings — any feelings — as your ally.

If you put in the time and effort, you can learn how to effectively manage your emotions

Emotional control begins and ends with your ability to exercise self-control.

Self-regulation refers to the capacity to be aware of one's own thoughts, feelings, and emotions and to make deliberate decisions about how one will respond in a way that is beneficial for both oneself and others.

Emotional control is a skill that may be acquired through practice. According to a number of studies, including one that will be published in 2020, it begins to take shape during childhood as a result of your interaction with your key caregivers. In point of fact, we are not born with the ability to comfort ourselves. The process of restoring equilibrium is referred to as co-regulation, and it is dependent on the neural systems of our caregivers.

When we are unsettled and out of control as infants, it can be helpful to lie on the chest of a caregiver and try to synchronize our breathing with theirs in order to feel more at ease. The way in which our primary caregivers manage their own emotions, as well as the messages they convey to us about how we should understand and deal with our own feelings, can have a significant influence on how we come to terms with our own feelings and on whether or not we believe we are capable of doing so. It's possible that adolescents and adults who lacked a supporting environment in their early infancy may have a harder time learning how to control their emotions as they get older. Don't give up hope if any of these things ring familiar to you. There are a few different approaches that could be helpful.

Take a few deep breaths

As the "fight, flight, or freeze" response kicks into high gear when you feel emotionally overwhelmed, it is impossible to think logically and feel your emotions at the same time. This is because of how the fight, flight, or freeze response works.

Your heart rate is most likely increasing, the blood flow to your digestive tract and kidneys is decreasing, and your adrenaline levels are beginning to rise. It is extremely challenging, if not impossible, to comprehend what other people are saying when you are in this state, let alone be conscious of your own ideas and feelings. You are, in essence, in the mode of survival in response to a perceived threat.

Breathwork may be of assistance. The parasympathetic nervous system, often known as your "rest-and-digest mode," is activated when you practice deep breathing, according to research conducted in 2018. This mode enables your body to relax and regain its equilibrium.

A calming effect on the senses

When your feelings are running high, it might be difficult to feel as like you are present in your body or the world around you physically. If it is at all possible, you should make an effort to tune into your five senses so that you can remain grounded. This can include any one of a variety of grounding tactics, such as spraying cold water on your face, singing or humming, or employing a method known as progressive muscular relaxation. After you have finished the exercise, you will have provided yourself with a distraction from the source of your stress, which will allow your parasympathetic nervous system to kick in and relieve some of your tension.

Activities that promote mindfulness

A study published in 2019 found that participants who meditated daily for eight weeks for a total of thirteen minutes saw improvements in their mood as well as greater control over their emotions. It has been found that practicing mindfulness can actually affect the matter in your brain. Because of something called neuroplasticity, our brains have the ability to alter, grow, and adapt in response to the activities that we put them through.

If sitting still and focusing your attention inward isn't your thing, you could try something else like yoga, tai chi, gardening, or forest bathing instead.

Get in the habit of accepting your feelings

We have a tendency to assign "negative" or "bad" connotations to our feelings far too frequently. When you're already feeling emotionally charged, this can add another layer of shame or guilt on top of what you're currently feeling. Rather than approaching your emotions from a place of judgment, you might find it useful to approach them from a place of inquiry instead. This perspective, also known as the state of letting sentiments to ebb and flow like the tide, is referred to as the "observer" mindset.

When you become aware of the emergence of your feelings, it can be helpful to have a conversation with yourself along the lines of "Isn't that interesting?" I find myself becoming enraged. I accept that it is in this space, and I will make it through this challenge.

Put your opinions up for debate

If you are experiencing emotional pain as a result of irrational beliefs, you might find it beneficial to confront such thoughts by engaging in cognitive reappraisal (changing the narrative).

Consult with a trained professional

It is not necessary for you to go through this ordeal by yourself. Reaching out for support from a therapist could be something that you find to be helpful. Due to the fact that we are unable to perceive the big picture while we are activated, therapy is an excellent place to work on this issue. We are only getting a very small glimpse of it at this point. Your therapist will be able to assist you in identifying your triggers and working through any unresolved traumatic experiences that may be adding fuel to the fire.

6. Mindfulness Tools & Exercises to Take Control of Your Life

These days, children have a lot of reasons to feel stressed out. The levels of stress experienced by students in the United States are on the rise. This can be attributed to a variety of factors, including increased academic pressure and increased participation in extracurricular activities, as well as interpersonal conflicts and even acts of violence that occur on campus. Children have increased levels of stress as a direct result of environmental issues such as climate change. It has been found that 61% of teenagers feel pressure to do well in school while another 29 percent say they are under a lot of pressure to appear a specific way and blend in with their peers. In addition, there is a lot of pressure to be active in athletics, to take part in extracurricular activities, and to get into a reputable institution. Dealing with the mundane aspects of day-to-day existence can be quite taxing and upsetting.

When you consider all of these strains and tensions, in addition to the rising incidence of anxiety and depression among adolescents, it is not surprise that promoting mental health has become a primary concern for both parents and teachers. Mindfulness is gaining popularity as a technique that can assist adolescents in overcoming the detrimental effects of the stresses and emotions that are present in their daily lives.

What Does It Mean to Be Mindful?

To put it in the simplest words possible, practicing mindfulness involves giving one object one's undivided attention and letting go of all other thoughts in the present now. It involves easing up on the pace and truly paying attention to what you are doing, even if it only entails concentrating on your breath at first. Being mindful is the antithesis of being able to multitask effectively.

Practicing mindfulness teaches children and teenagers how to relax, spend their time, and concentrate on something without feeling rushed or tense in the process. Breathing techniques, mental imagery, becoming aware of sensations in the body, and general relaxation are typically included in a mindfulness meditation session.

How Being Mindful Can Be Helpful

When confronted with anything challenging in their lives, children and adolescents can better manage their feelings of helplessness and anger by developing the skill of practicing mindfulness. It can also be employed in situations in which the person needs to concentrate on one item in particular and not let any distractions cause them to stray from their goal. Being attentive is a skill that, with practice, can be developed further and further by children and adolescents.

In addition to that, it is effective. In point of fact, studies have shown that practicing mindfulness can enhance attention spans for virtually everyone. This includes young individuals with ADHD, who frequently struggle to pay attention to what's going on around them. People who learn to practice mindfulness tend to be better at paying attention to what's going on around them and less easily distracted. Individuals who practice mindfulness are also better able to maintain composure in the face of adversity, resist being overly agitated, improve their ability to get along with people, and become more patient. It can even have an effect on a child's ability to learn, as well as assist them become better listeners and make them feel happier overall.

Teenage years are crucial periods in a young person's development, although they differ significantly from one another. What takes place during these stages of their lives will serve as the groundwork for their psychological well-being in the years to come.

Students who practice mindfulness are better able to understand how to halt in a variety of settings and respond in a way that is deliberate rather than simply reacting. This ability is especially helpful in situations in which they are confronted with problems or come into contact with children who bully others.

It shouldn't come as a surprise that teaching children and teenagers how to deal with stress, learn to control their feelings, concentrate on the work at hand, and cultivate a more optimistic attitude on life may be accomplished through the practice of mindfulness.

When children and adolescents practice mindfulness, they also get a deeper comprehension of how their own brains function. There is a possibility that kids will develop an interest in learning more about the workings of their own thoughts and the reasons for their own emotions. The practice of mindfulness has been found to bring a variety of mental, emotional, and social advantages when it is used in educational settings by researchers.

Cognitive Benefits

It has been demonstrated through research that teaching children mindfulness can have a positive effect on their cognitive abilities, particularly the executive tasks that are carried out by the brain. Executive functions are in charge of a person's capacity to focus, switch focus, organize information, remember details, and plan.

In point of fact, a study that was conducted with third-grade kids over the course of 2 months found that when a mindfulness program was introduced in the school, the students exhibited improvements in terms of regulating their actions and focusing on the job at hand when compared to a control group that did not engage in a mindfulness program. This was discovered in comparison to students who were assigned to the group that did not participate in a mindfulness program.

In the meantime, a different study discovered that elementary school students who participated in a mindfulness program that lasted for twenty-four weeks achieved higher scores on attention-based activities than other students in their school. Similarly, a study conducted on preschoolers discovered that pupils who participated in a mindfulness curriculum performed higher on exams measuring academic performance. In addition to this, they demonstrated a bigger improvement in areas that are predictive of their future academic achievement.

Advantages to One's Mood

Emotional wellness, often known as a feeling of positivity and overall happiness, is an essential component of a child's development throughout their lifetime. Not only is it the foundation of mental health, but it can also help prevent mental health problems such as anxiety, stress, depression, challenges with one's self-esteem, and problems with one's ability to communicate with others.

In general, practicing mindfulness or taking part in activities that emphasize mindfulness can help students not just better manage the stress in their lives but also improve their overall feeling of well-being. One study, for instance, discovered that after taking part in a mindfulness training, students were significantly more likely to report feeling optimistic about their lives. Another study indicated that preteens who participated in a mindfulness and stress-reduction program for five weeks reported feeling calmer, getting better sleep, and having an elevated sense of well-being compared to preteens who did not participate in the program.

Social Benefits

Learning, comprehension, and the overall climate of the school can be negatively impacted when there is difficulty interacting and talking with others. However, it has been demonstrated that participating in mindfulness programs can strengthen these skills and contribute to favorable effects within the school.

A five-week mindfulness program at an elementary school, for example, resulted in increased involvement in classroom activities. In the meantime, a mindfulness program at a high school was helping to foster mutual respect and care among students, which contributed to an overall improvement in the climate of the school.

Other Benefits

Research has indicated that practicing mindfulness can improve a child's or teen's ability to self-regulate their emotions, as well as their capacity for compassion and empathy. It is also commonly regarded as a helpful treatment for persons of all ages who struggle with aggressive behavior, attention deficit hyperactivity disorder (ADHD), or other mental health issues such as anxiety. And also has the potential to be utilized to reduce the agonizing impacts of being bullied.

The practice of mindfulness can also be utilized as a method to improve one's self-concept, boost planning abilities, and exercise better impulse control. When implemented correctly in educational settings, mindfulness has the potential to enhance students' attendance, lower instances of bullying in the classroom, and cut down on the number of times they have to go to the principal's office.

In general, the goal of teaching children and teenagers mindfulness is to get them to examine their own thoughts and actions and figure out how to improve their decision-making. They are no longer merely reacting to the things that are happening in their surroundings; rather, they are responding to these things in ways that are intelligent and purposeful.

In the end, when children and adolescents grow to realize that they can be in control of their ideas, feelings, and behaviors, not only do they feel more in charge of their decision-making processes, but they also make better choices.

Simple Methods for Incorporating Mindfulness Into Everyday Life

How frequently do you rush out the door and into your day without even giving any thought to how you would like things to go? Things and people can quickly irritate you to the point that you respond unexpectedly, such as becoming irritated or angry when they offend your sensitivities.

You are not required to continue behaving in this manner. It is possible to make your days more enjoyable and more in line with how you would like them to be by pausing for a few minutes at various points during the day to engage in the practice of mindfulness.

Wake up mindfully and begin with the end in mind

The term "intention" refers to the fundamental reason that lies behind all that we think, say, and do. When we act in ways that were not what we intended, there is a disconnect, from the perspective of the brain, between the faster, unconscious impulses of the lower brain centers and the slower, conscious, wiser abilities of the higher centers like the pre-frontal cortex. This disconnect causes us to behave in ways that were not what we intended.

This method can help you align your higher-order cognitive processes with the more primal emotional needs of your brain's lower centers. Given that the unconscious brain is responsible for the majority of our decision-making and behaviors, this is an extremely useful skill to have. In addition to the assurance of one's own well-being, these include reasons such as reward, connection, purpose, self-identity, and fundamental principles.

Setting a goal and recalling those earliest impulses can aid in the development of a stronger connection between both the lower and upper centers. Doing this can make your day better and increase the likelihood that your words, actions, and responses—especially in tough situations—will be so much more attentive and sympathetic.

To get the most out of this routine, you should perform it first thing in the morning, preferably before checking your phone or email.

1. As soon as you open your eyes, take a relaxing seat in either your bed or a chair. Put your eyes closed and bring your awareness to the feelings that arise from your seated body. Be sure that your spine is aligned properly, but don't let it get rigid.

2. Inhale slowly and deeply for three full breaths to help you relax. Breathe in deeply and exhale through your mouth. 3. Perform this step three times more. Pay attention to how your chest and abdomen expand and contract as you exhale once you've established a regular breathing rate for yourself.

3. Ponder this question aloud: "What do I want to accomplish today?" When you are thinking about the different people and activities that you will be participating in, use these questions

as a guide to help you answer that question. Ask yourself: "How can I make the most of today's opportunities to have an impact? Which aspect of my mental makeup do I wish to improve upon and cultivate? In order to take better care of myself, what do I need to do? How can I be more empathetic to others and to myself when I'm going through challenging times? How can I make myself feel more connected to others and more fulfilled?"

4. Determine what you want to get out of the day. For instance, you could say something like, "Today, I will be nice to myself; be patient with others; give generously; stay grounded; persevere; have fun; eat well," or you could say anything else that you consider to be significant.

5. At various points during the day, check in with who you are. Put a pause in what you're doing, take a deep breath, and think about your objective. Become increasingly aware of the effects that focusing on your goals for each day has on the quality of your interactions with others, the relationships you have, and the feelings you experience.

Enjoy every bite you take when you eat mindfully

It is not difficult to simplify the experience of eating to the sensations of biting, chewing, and swallowing. Who among us hasn't gotten halfway through a platter of food before realizing what they're doing? However, eating is one of the most joyful activities that we, as humans, get to partake in, and if we do so consciously, we can transform the act of eating into a much more fulfilling one, one that satisfies not only the need for sustenance but also other, subtler senses and desires. We are able to satisfy all of our appetites if we focus our complete attention on our bodies and determine what it is that we need most to eat. Give this a try:

1. Take a breath before you start eating. We frequently jump from one work to the next without pausing for a moment or taking a breath in between. We are able to slow down and make a smoother transition into our meals if we take a moment to pause periodically. Before beginning your meal, bring your focus within by shutting your eyes, and then take eight to ten calm, deep breaths in and out of your stomach. Do this for the duration of the breathing exercise.

2. Pay attention to your bodily cues. Following the inhalation, direct your attention to the feelings that are occurring in your

abdominal region. Asking yourself, "How hungry am I?" on a scale where 1 indicates that you don't feel any bodily sense of hunger and 10 indicates that you are very hungry is a good way to gauge your hunger level. What kinds of bodily sensations, such as a growling stomach, shakiness, a lack of desire to eat, or an empty feeling in your stomach, can help you determine whether or not you are hungry? Try not to focus about the time or the last time you ate, and instead pay attention to what your body is telling you rather than what your brain are telling you.

3. Allow your hunger to guide what you eat. Now that you are more aware of how hungry you are, you are in a better position to make more thoughtful decisions regarding the food you consume, when you eat it, and how much you eat. You can better tune in to your true requirements by engaging in this straightforward activity.

4. Practice calm eating. When you sit down for your next meal, make sure to take your time and focus on deep breathing while you eat. If you aren't able to relax, you won't be able to properly digest or enjoy your food as much.

5. If you don't enjoy it, there's no reason to consume it. Take your first three bites slowly and deliberately, focusing on the taste, flavors, and textures of the food as well as the amount of pleasure you are deriving from it. When deciding what to eat,

put some thought into it and choose something that you genuinely enjoy.

Rewiring Your Brain Through Mindful Pauses

It is believed that 95 percent of our conduct is carried out on autopilot, which is a phenomenon that I refer to as "speed brain." Because neural networks are the foundation of all of our routines, they transform the millions of sensory inputs that we receive every second into more manageable shortcuts, allowing us to function normally in this chaotic world. These default brain impulses are comparable to signaling superhighways; they are so effective at what they do that they frequently compel us to revert to past habits before we are able to recall what it was that we had intended to do instead.

The practice of mindfulness, sometimes known as "slow brain," is the polar opposite of these activities. It's not autopilot; it's executive control, and it enables conscious acts, willpower, and decisions. However, that requires a lot of practice. The more we engage the more primitive parts of our brain, the more robust they become. We activate our grey matter, which is full of newly sprung neurons that have not yet been groomed for the quick brain, every time we do something that is purposeful and new. This is because neuroplasticity is stimulated whenever we do something new.

However, herein lies the rub. Although the slower part of my brain is aware of what's best for me, the faster part of my brain is driving me to take shortcuts through life. The question now is how we may train ourselves to be conscious at the precise moment when we most require it. The concept known as "behavior design" enters the picture at this point. It's a method to make your slow brain the one in control of the situation. There are two approaches to this problem: first, one can try to slow down the rapid brain by placing barriers in its path; second, one can try to seize control of the situation by eliminating obstacles from the path of the slow brain.

However, it takes some effort to shift the balance in order to provide your slow brain with additional power. Here are several different approaches to take to get started.

1. Make a hasty decision on what you wish to do. If you want to do some yoga or meditate, place your meditation cushion or yoga mat in the middle of your floor so that you won't be able to miss it as you walk by.

2. You should frequently revise your triggers. Let's say you make the decision to utilize post-it notes as a way to remind yourself of a new goal or objective. It's possible that this will work for about a week, but eventually, your lazy brain and old routines

will take over again. Try composing new notes to yourself; make them amusing or add variation to increase the likelihood that you will remember them.

3. Develop original recurring formats. You could find it helpful to set up a sequence of "If this, then that" messages as a way to establish simple reminders for yourself to go into slow brain mode. Even if the door to your office is closed, you can still practice mindfulness by saying something like, "If the door is open, take a deep breath." Or, "When the phone rings, pause for a moment before picking it up." Your habitual, habitual brain will become stronger with every conscious action you take to shift into mindfulness.

Your Mind and Your Muscles Will Wake Up When You Do This Mindful Workout

What are some of the similarities between activities such as riding a bike, lifting weights, and working up a sweat on a treadmill? One way in which each might be utilized is as a form of mindfulness practice. Tango dancing, swimming, or any other form of physical activity can help you transform your mindset from one of being busy and preoccupied to one of being able and confident, no matter what you're doing. This is because you can move and breathe in a way that not only gets your heart rate up and invigorates every cell in your body.

Ready? You will be able to better coordinate your body, mind, and neurological system by following these procedures, which are applicable to any activity. You will become better able to direct all of your focus toward the task at hand as you continue to perform what you are doing now.

1. Have a crystal clear vision of your end goal. Bring purpose to the action you are performing, such as tying your shoes or putting on your gardening gloves, by actively imagining in your mind how you would like to direct your session. You may tell yourself as you get on your bike, "I am going to take a few deep breaths and focus on the experience of the breeze, the sun, and the passing countryside." You may tell yourself as you step into the water, "From this point on, I'm going to pay attention to each stroke, as well as the sound and sensation of the water all around me."

2. Get your body ready (5 minutes). You may try doing jumping jacks or stretching, for example, and focus on synchronizing the rhythm of your breath with the action that you are doing. Moving to a rhythmic beat will cause your nervous system and heart rate to harmonize with your brain's activity.

3. Get into a comfortable routine (10 to 15 minutes). Increase the difficulty of the exercise while maintaining control of your breathing and movement throughout. If you find that you are having difficulty doing this, all you need to do is concentrate on your breathing for a few minutes. You'll get into a good rhythm at some point.

4. Put yourself to the test (10 to 15 minutes). Depending on what you are doing, try increasing the speed, the number of repetitions, or the weight that you are lifting. Take note of how aware and vibrant you feel whenever you push yourself to your limits.

5. Calm yourself down (5 minutes). Bring yourself to a complete stop by gradually slowing down your pace until you reach it. Take note of how your body currently feels. Take in your surroundings and relax.

6. Rest (5 minutes). Recognize in a calm and collected manner the symphony of sensations that is flowing in and around you. Get in the habit of putting words to what your body is telling you. There is a good chance that you will feel wide awake and energized from head to toe.

When you're behind the wheel, practice mindful driving by keeping a level head and not going completely insane

When combined, high traffic and irritable drivers are a perfect storm for setting off the "fight or flight" reaction. Because of this, incidents of road rage and increased stress levels occur, while people's ability to reason is overcome. The more stressful the traffic, the more stressful the situation. My city, Los Angeles, is known for having some of the worst traffic in the area as well as some of the most inconsiderate drivers. The stakes are high, tempers are flaring, and the tires are squealing.

However, such circumstance doesn't have to persist. In point of fact, even the most frustrating traffic jam can be a golden opportunity to strengthen your mindfulness muscle, deepen your sense of connection to others, and regain some equilibrium and perspective in your life.

The following are the stages of a basic driving exercise that I've been doing for some time now behind the wheel. It's amazing how well it can work, in my experience.

1. To begin, draw a long and slow breath in. This piece of advice, which is deceptively straightforward despite its depth, can help you take in more oxygen and create greater distance between

the stress-inducing stimulus of the traffic and the response of your body to that stress. Perspective and options are both contained inside this space.

2. Determine what it is that you require. It's possible that in that same instant, you require some relief, the ability to feel safe and at ease, or all three. Gaining an understanding of what you require will help you achieve equilibrium.

3. Recognize your own requirements and meet them. You can scan your body for any tension (which is not a terrible thing to do while driving, in any case), then soften any tension you find or change your body as necessary in order to get the relaxation that you require. You may sprinkle in some self-compassionate lines here and there, such as "May I be at ease, may I feel protected, may I be joyful."

4. Take a look around you and realize that every other driver is in the same boat as you are. On the road, everyone's goal is the same as yours: to feel secure, to have a sense of relaxation, and to enjoy themselves to the fullest. There is a good chance that you will observe a number of other drivers who appear to be somewhat irritated; however, there is also a chance that you will observe another driver who is singing or genuinely smiling, and this will immediately alleviate some of the stress that you are experiencing. You are able to extend to all of them the same

wish that you have just made for yourself, which is that "may you feel at peace, may you feel protected, and may you be happy."

5. Take a few more long, slow breaths. You may completely alter your state of mind in less than a minute by putting these straightforward strategies into action. When you start to feel annoyed by the increasing volume of traffic, choose whatever it is that you need to improve and provide that situation to other people. As a way of ensuring your own safety and the safety of others, simply say, "May I, you, and every one of us be safe." Inhale, exhale, you've just planted the seed for someone else's happiness.

Other Fun Mindfulness Techniques

The Meditation on the Observer

The Observer Meditation is an important component of acceptance and commitment therapy (ACT), another form of psychotherapy in which mindfulness plays a significant role. It investigates the question of why it is beneficial to detach from our own internal thoughts and feelings.

Taking on the role of an observer can assist us in creating some separation between who we are and the problematic aspects of our lives with which we may be over identifying. To get started with the activity, please follow these steps:

Listen to the play as you find a position that allows you to sit comfortably

Allow yourself to get comfortable in your body as well as your head.

You should make an effort to let go of your thoughts and rid your mind of its normal concerns.

First and foremost, direct your attention on the space in which you currently find yourself. Imagine looking in on yourself from the outside as you sit, just as someone on the outside would. After then, bring your focus inward, into the surface of your skin. While you are seated in the chair, you should make an effort to feel your skin.

It may help to shift your concentration toward any physical feelings you are having if you try to imagine the form that your skin is producing when it comes into touch with the chair while you are sitting there. As you experience each one, you must first recognize its presence before allowing your consciousness to release its grasp on it and proceed with its natural progression.

If you notice that certain feelings are emerging, acknowledge them and make room for them in your life. Then, direct your focus back to the part of you that is the observer; your emotions and ideas are present, but you are distinct from them and simply noticing them. This is what we mean when we say "Observe you."

This activity can be performed for as long as the participant sees fit, and there are a number of stages that can be completed that will assist the participant become more skilled at being an observer of themselves. Because of our natural propensity to respond to and be too identified by the emotions that we experience, this is not an easy exercise to complete at first.

If you find that it is difficult to get out of your own thoughts and body, you might find it helpful to try practicing the self-compassion pause first in order to ease yourself into the experience. Entering a separate mode that enables you to take a step back from both yourself and the experiences you're having is the objective of the process of invoking the Observing Self. On the other hand, at the same time, you are connecting with a more fundamental aspect of yourself that is untouched by the fluctuating emotions.

Five Senses Exercise

This activity, which is referred to as "five senses," offers directions on how to practice mindfulness more rapidly in almost any circumstance. All that is required is for you to pay attention to anything that you are perceiving with each of your five senses. Practice your use of the five senses in the following order:

Take note of these five things that are in plain view.

Take a moment to look at your surroundings, and draw your attention to five different objects that you may observe. Choose anything that you would not ordinarily pay attention to, such as a shadow or a little crack in the concrete.

Take note of these four things that you can get a sense of.

Raise your awareness of four things that you are currently sensing, such as the sensation of the breeze on your skin, the surface of the table your hands are resting on, or the texture of the pants you are wearing.

Take note of these three items that can be heard.

Look around, and pay attention to these 3 things that you perceive in the distance: This could be a bird's chirp, a refrigerator's hum, or the subtle rumble of nearby traffic.

Take note of the two odors that are present.

Bring to the forefront of your attention odors that you normally ignore, regardless of whether they are pleasurable or unpleasant. If you are outside, the wind may be carrying the scent of pine trees, or it may be transporting the aroma of a fast-food restaurant that is located across the street.

Take note of one thing that can be tasted.

Your attention should be focused on one thing that you can taste right now, in this very instant. You may take a swig of a drink, chew on a piece of gum, eat something, concentrate on the taste that is already present in your mouth, or simply just open your mouth and try to detect a flavor in the air.

You can immediately enter a state of mindfulness by performing this practice, which is short and not very difficult. You can perform the 5 senses technique to focus on the present now even if you have few minutes to spare, or if you don't really have access to body scans or worksheets. This is especially helpful in situations where you don't have much time to spare.

The Method of Contemplatively Strolling Down the Street

Our capacity to watch our thoughts, feelings, and sensations without attempting to fix, hide, or otherwise solve them is one of the fundamental processes that can be affected by the practice of mindfulness. This awareness opens up the possibility of making a choice between acting on impulses or taking action, which can assist in the development of abilities for dealing with adversity and beneficial changes in behavior.

The first part of this intervention involves visualizing a situation in which the individual in question is making their way down a street they are familiar with when they suddenly look up and recognize someone who is standing on the other side of the street. They give each other a wave, but the other individual doesn't acknowledge it and keeps walking past them without stopping.

In the second stage of the method, a series of questions are posed to you in order to stimulate introspection. These questions are as follows:

1. While you were visualizing, were any of your thoughts brought to your attention?

2. While you were visualizing, were you aware of any of the feelings that you were experiencing?

Observe how their conduct is affected by the sequence of thoughts and feelings that came up, whether the practice was helpful, and for any closing notes in the 3rd stage of the process.

The Reflective Pause of Three Minutes

This activity, in contrast to others such as a body scan or meditation, may be completed in a short amount of time and is helpful in launching a mindfulness practice.

During practices like meditation and the body scan, one's mind will frequently wander, and it can be difficult to keep one's thoughts in check and maintain mental clarity. This final exercise of the 3-Minute Breathing Space can be the ideal method for individuals who lead hectic lives and have active minds. The workout is divided into three parts, with one component occurring every minute, and it goes as follows:

The first minute is spent trying to answer the question "how am I doing right now?" by concentrating on the emotions, ideas, and sensations that come up during this time and coming up with words and phrases to describe them.

The second minute is dedicated to maintaining awareness of the breath throughout the entire minute.

The final minute is spent directing attention away from the breath and towards the rest of the body, with the goal of becoming more aware of the ways in which your breathing affects other parts of your body.

Maintaining mental stillness can be somewhat difficult, since one will frequently be confronted with thoughts. The goal here is not to prevent them from entering your mind; rather, it is to allow them entrance before allowing them to leave again. Just try to keep an eye on them.

All of the exercises listed above can be done by you, your customers, and even in group situations. All client groups can benefit from them, but some will benefit more than others, so it is often necessary to try things out with an open mind.

The most important thing to remember about mindfulness is that it is a mental activity that takes time to observe results from. Persistence, self-compassion, and a willingness to adapt to new tactics and therapies are the keys to success.

Introducing Dialectical Behavioral Therapy

Cognitive-behavioral therapy known as Dialectical Behavioral Therapy (DBT) has been shown to be effective in treating borderline personality disordered persons. The Dialectical Behavioral Therapy process is outlined as follows:

People with serious mental health disorders typically engage in activities that risk their life, which is why DBT treatment focuses on addressing these behaviors first.

DBT counselors work to eradicate behaviors that impede therapy, such as the refusal to pursue the DBT goals, the absence of regular therapy appointments;

In the second phase of treatment, DBT therapists work to rectify the client's unproductive relationships, communication issues, and bad financial decisions.
In DBT, mindfulness is a key skill because it helps clients become aware of their own feelings and thoughts. [10]

The Effectiveness of Dialectical Behavioural Therapy-Mindfulness

There has been research into the effectiveness of Dialectical Behavioral Therapy-Mindfulness (DBTM) training as an addition to standard psychiatric care. The "what" and "how" abilities of mindfulness were the subject of a module designed to help customers acquire the "wise mind.". [11]

Simple Mindfulness Exercises from Dialectical Behavioural Therapy

Observe a Leaf for Five Minutes

As an adjunct to normal mental health treatment, researchers have looked into the effectiveness of Dialectical Behavioral Therapy-Mindfulness (DBTM) training. Customers who purchased a module on mindfulness' "what" and "how" capabilities were able to do so.

Mindful Eating for Four Minutes

This activity requires a deliberate approach to eating. Pay close attention to what you're holding and how it feels in your hands. After you've taken in the appearance of the object in terms of its weight, color, and so on, it's time to focus on how it smells. After that, you may finally move on to eating, but this time you should take your time and pay close attention to what you're doing. Take note of the flavor as well as the sensation it produces on your tongue. This practice could help you find new experiences with foods that are already familiar to you.

Spend the next fifteen minutes observing your thoughts

The purpose of this exercise, which is fundamental to the practice of mindfulness, is to simply heighten your awareness of your own thoughts. To begin, find a comfortable posture (sitting or lying down) and make an effort to release any and all tension that may be present in your body. First, bring your attention to the sensations occurring in your breathing; second, observe how it feels to be in your body; and third, consider what is going through your mind.

Be conscious of the things that go through your mind, but fight the temptation to categorize or evaluate these thoughts.

Imagine them as a fleeting cloud that moves through the mental landscape of your mind.

If your mind wanders to follow an idea, notice whatever it was that captured your focus and gently guide your attention back to your thoughts.

Exercise in Mindfulness Utilizing a Bell for Five Minutes

In the first part of this workout, you are going to shut your eyes and concentrate on finding the cue. The moment you become aware of it, you should direct all of your attention to the sound and maintain this level of concentration until it disappears entirely. You will find that by engaging in this activity, you are better able to keep your feet firmly planted in the here and now.

7.   Practice Saying Yes

Recently, there has been a lot of discussion about being better at declining offers. The concept of creating more room and more time so that we can do the things we love, the things we want, or the things we feel like doing, rather than feeling pressured into saying "yes" or "maybe" to everyone who asks us for our time and attention. But when did giving an affirmative response turn into something so frowned upon?

Have you ever taken the time to reflect on how frequently you use the word "No"? Not only to things that have good reason to be rejected, but also to novel concepts, novel opportunities, and the opportunity to make unanticipated discoveries? Every time you tell life "No," you pass up an opportunity to learn and develop, to uncover a new facet of yourself or others, to learn something new, to try something you haven't tried before, to attempt something you haven't tried before, to discover something new. to begin anything new, whether it is a passion, a project, or even the path that your life should take.

You may not be able to accept every request that comes your way, but there is a good chance that you could accept more than you currently do. Pay attention to what you think. What do you respond with when someone invites you to join them in doing something that they enjoy doing but that you have never done before? Do you seize the opportunity to give it a shot? Or, do you respectfully decline their invitations, explaining that your time is too valuable to waste on anything for which you are unsure as to whether or not you will enjoy it in advance?

The process of learning and living are same. When you stop being curious about new things, you start to lose a little bit of your vitality each day. There is evidence in the scientific community that connections between brain cells can regenerate at any age if the cells are exercised. It's a matter of "use it or lose it" when it comes to your brain.

The Strength of Yes

The true nature of potential was one of the most significant concepts that I wished to convey to you. It is not one's intelligence, fortune, or power that determines success. The word "potential" means "possibility." Your potential is directly proportional to the number of options and routes open to you at any given moment. Because of this, every person possesses potential, but very little of it is ever put to use.

Imagine there are two persons. Martin is smart, but he prefers to stick to what he is already familiar with. Manuela is a naturally inquisitive person who enjoys challenging herself by engaging in novel experiences in order to better understand the world around her.

Move ahead in time a few years. Martin is acting in the same manner that he normally does. Even though he is in a strong position, he has not advanced. Manuela is keen to expand her knowledge and has experimented with a great number of novel concepts. Martin is in jeopardy of falling further and further behind since the world never stops moving. His meticulously constructed safety could be compromised at any moment by an unforeseen circumstance. If this is the case, he will discover that he has lost a significant portion of his self-assurance and ease of learning. Change will be imposed on him, and it is quite unlikely that he would adapt well to it. Alteration is something that Manuela views as usual. She may still have disappointments and failures, but she has developed the ability to grow from her mistakes and adapt well to shifting circumstances. Because she has put in so much work, she will have no trouble picking up new skills whenever she requires them.

The word "potential" means "possibility." You just have a few options in your life? Your potential is extremely limited. It can be increased by providing additional options. The only path forward is education. It is a fundamental rule of the natural world. The species that are most closely associated with a particular ecological niche are the ones that are at the greatest risk of extinction. The species that are able to adapt the best to their environments are the ones that will thrive regardless of the circumstances. Want proof? Take a look at all the pigeons and sparrows that are flying around you. Is there a significant chance that they will become extinct in the not-too-distant future? However, they are not strong birds like eagles, nor are they even intelligent birds like parrots. They are extremely malleable due to what they are.

Give it a shot. Say "Yes" to an opportunity that you would have normally declined. Experiment with new foods, listen to new music, and watch a movie that you would generally avoid. Experiment with acting in a new way. Even if you have a reputation for being timid, you should strive to strike up a conversation with interesting people. If you tend to be loud and outgoing, you can try being more reserved and observing what goes on around you while others grab the spotlight. You will acquire new knowledge regardless of the outcome. It's even possible that you'll stumble onto an excellent surprise. There is no need for this to be in any way dramatic. The important thing is not to hold yourself back or to stick with what you are already familiar with; rather, what counts is that you expose yourself to more of what life has to offer.

Many people go through their lives and careers under the false impression that there is just one option available to them. Because they never experiment with anything else, this proves that it is correct. However, the world is not a collection of laws to be obeyed or a checklist to be completed; rather, it is a gigantic and wonderful experiment. It depends entirely on you how actively you choose to participate in that experiment. The more closely you adhere to the same script, the less likely it is that you will uncover something that could be even more beneficial.

Fear of losing what they already have, regardless matter how flawed it may be, is what keeps most individuals back from moving forward. Just keep in mind that the experiment is under your direction the entire time. You can easily experiment with a minor adjustment just as readily as you can with a major one. And even if it doesn't work out the first time, you can always try it again later. The true danger lies in replying "No," as this puts an end to any possibility of something being done differently in the future.

The game-changing effects of Saying "yes"

The word "yes" is typically associated with positive connotations, including those of acceptance and affirmation. But not everybody is aware of how this one word, which is both simple and magical, may be used in the most effective way to change their lives. You did not misunderstand what was said. There are countless ways in which your life might be improved by increasing the frequency with which you use the word "yes."

When we come across anything that is unusual and out of the ordinary, our first inclination is to avoid it or express that we disapprove of it. Because our brains are wired to prioritize the preservation of our safety, we have a tendency to be slow to embrace new information. On the other hand, during that process, our brains do not make it easy for us to take chances or experience new things. Simply allowing oneself to participate in novel activities that contribute to our personal development requires only a simple "yes." Because "Growth comes outside of one's comfort zone," saying "yes" involves allowing oneself to step outside of one's safe and familiar environment.

If, on the other hand, we use the word "no" more frequently, it indicates that we are placing restrictions on ourselves and shutting the door on fresh chances for personal development. According to a well-known proverb, "Saying 'Yes' can alter your life for the better and inspire others to do the same," saying "Yes" can have both of these effects.

Let's take a look at the ways in which simply answering "yes" can transform our life.

Accepting the benefits of possibilities

Yes to opportunity is the most important "yes" that you need to learn to say, therefore practice it often. It is not only about seizing the opportunities that are presented to you right now, but also about being prepared to seize the opportunities that may come your way at any time. In addition to that, it is about looking for possibilities that are subtly tapping on the door. In addition to this, it is important to seize opportunities whenever you get the chance.

There are no excuses for not taking advantage of every opportunity that comes your way, such as claiming that "the moment is right" or "I'm not good enough." mostly due to the fact that you can never be sure when the next one will come to your door. Additionally, if you do not test the limits of your abilities, you will never know how far you can go. Therefore, do not sit about waiting for the right moment to act. You may begin wherever you are and with whatever you have. The secret to being successful is to get started before you are completely prepared.

In contrast, if you turn off new opportunities, it is unlikely that you will investigate what lies in store for you in the future. It is a form of failure in and of itself to refuse to pursue fresh chances due to apprehensions about failing or fear of doing so. Fear itself is the only thing that should be feared.

Accepting and even seeking out challenges

Although it might be counterintuitive, the ultimate demonstration of strength that one can give is to accept obstacles with a positive attitude. In addition, this is the most important component in preparing you to deal with challenging circumstances later on in your life. Keep in mind that there will always be challenges in front of you on the path to achievement. The manner in which an individual deals with problems is what divides winners from those who give up.

We need to give "yes" credit for being the tool that helped us remodel our lives. If there is something that will challenge you and drive you to step outside of your comfort zone, you should make it a point to say yes to it. Whether you do so gladly or unwillingly, accept them. And everything will work out beautifully. You will be able to overcome your fear of whatever it was that was making you anxious if you just face it head on and do it. Things won't appear to be any more terrifying. Your anxiety in social situations, as well as your stage fright and dread of public speaking, will completely disappear.

You can only reach your full potential if you accept difficulties and rise to meet them. This gives you the ability to understand what you are capable of doing and how your skills can be expanded.

Accepting what your gut tells you to do

Trusting one's instincts and following through on them is what is meant by "giving in" to one's intuition. Your intrinsic leaning or predisposition toward a specific concept, item, event, or conclusion is referred to as intuition. Without engaging in a great deal of logical deliberation, this internal compass acts as a guide that enables you to arrive at better decisions in your own self-interest more quickly.

While it's true that being open to new experiences and chances is one of the benefits of always going with your gut and saying yes, there are occasions when doing so can take you in directions that aren't necessarily in your best interest. When we are faced with a situation like this, we must rely on our intuition. Be aware, too, that the 'no' that your intuition gives you is not the same as the 'no' that you give to fresh prospects for advancement because you lack the drive or the efficiency to pursue them.

This distinction is one that must be discovered by having the bravery to put in the necessary work. In order for us to be able to give more meaningful responses when we say "yes," we need to learn when to say "yes" and when to say "no." In situations like this, our intuition is the most reliable source of information. Simply gaining trust in this is all that is required of us to learn.

Choosing to accept in order to behave with assurance

Saying "yes" more frequently is the most important component that contributes to a strong and confident outlook. You will find that you have more opportunities available to you if you accept communication. You are able to form relationships with new people and gain knowledge of new opportunities that you would not have had otherwise. Even yet, this is not a step-by-step process. The beginning is going to be challenging. You experience feelings of anxiety before to showing up. It's possible that you'll make some clumsy statements. But if you make a habit of being open to new connections and conversations at all times, you will inevitably develop more self-assurance. This one action will introduce you to fresh opportunities and thoughts that you were previously unaware even existed. If you answer "Yes," you will be able to take more chances, which will ultimately lead to an expansion of your knowledge and understanding.

Accepting the challenge to outperform

Your chances of becoming successful will improve if you answer "yes" to the challenge of outperforming your previous self. Not only does this make it possible for other people to have faith in you, but it also demonstrates that you are a respectable human being. Additionally, by answering "yes," you are agreeing to be responsible to yourself. Because once you make a commitment to other people and to yourself, you figure out ways to keep that commitment regardless. This opens the door for innovation as well as other approaches to accomplishing more. Because of this, you may now say, "I did it," instead of "It seems impossible." As time goes on, you will develop greater habits of productivity and tenacity as a result of going through this process.

Giving Your Emotions and Feelings the "Yes" They Deserve

It is very normal for feelings to come and go. This flow can be a calm stream at times, but it can also be a roaring torrent at other times. Some youngsters are able to express their feelings openly, while others experience difficulties expressing their feelings from a young age onward. Adolescence and adulthood, on the other hand, are when the emotional faucet starts to get clogged.

As we get older, we tend to become better at stuffing down our feelings, and there are a lot of different reasons for this. Fear of allowing themselves to fully express their feelings is one of the most prevalent reasons cited by those who confide in me that they bottle up their feelings. People are afraid of letting their feelings out, of feeling out of control, and of having to live with the consequences of their actions. Therefore, how can we acquire the skill of expressing our feelings in a protected manner so that we do not come to regret the consequences of our actions?

It's possible that the first thing we need to do is acknowledge and accept our feelings. Welcoming the good, the terrible, and the ugly of them all is important. They should not be denied. Give yourself the go-ahead to feel whatever you're feeling and to express it.

Next, ensure that you give yourself the necessary time and space to feel and express the feelings that you are experiencing. In the middle of the crisis at work, it's unlikely that this will be possible. No issue. Hold off on investigating your emotions and feelings until you are in an environment in which you believe it is safe to do so. Bring the memory of the event that triggered the sentiments and emotions into the area you've designated for exploration and re-experiencing. If you give yourself permission to perform this work on the same day that the emotions and feelings are first experienced, there is a good chance that you won't have any trouble bringing them back up to the surface later on.

The most essential thing to remember is to 'feel' your way into and out of your thoughts and feelings when you are in a safe environment. Let things take its natural course. Perhaps it will be through the use of writing or painting or movement of the body. It's important to let your sentiments and emotions flow in whichever way works best for you in terms of reliving, reenacting, acting out, expressing, releasing, and cleansing your stored energy.

It's probable that dealing with your sentiments and emotions in just one sitting won't be enough. Be patient. It's possible that you'll want to or feel the need to seek the perspective of a trusted friend, confidant, or even a trained professional while you go through this experience. Carry out the necessary steps. When you engage in this process of self-care on a regular basis, it will become easier for you to let your sentiments and emotions flow freely, rather than repressing or stifling them.

8. Navigate Social Stress

When feelings of exhaustion, stress, and mental exhaustion begin to cloud one's thinking, it is essential to identify the source of these feelings and take direct action to address them. There are millions of articles that discuss how stress can negatively affect a person's mental health and overall welfare. However, what about the factors that contribute to stress? Do a person's social surroundings play a role? It very certainly does, and we refer to this phenomenon as social stress. In the following paragraphs, we will cover social stress, including what it is, what it is not, and how to deal with this sensation, which frequently plays a large role in the job, at home, and within relationships.

The Difference Between Social Stress and Social Anxiety

What exactly is the societal pressure? It is common practice to describe social stress as actions and events that are social in origin but are linked to physical and psychological strain for the individual. This stress may come from friendship groups, challenging work conditions, academic clubs, or severe family situations. It may also come from academic clubs. A person who suffers from social anxiety, on the other hand, experiences substantial levels of worry, self-consciousness, and embarrassment during ordinary encounters. This is due to the individual's fear of being examined or assessed harshly by other people. Fear and worry can lead to avoidance, which can have a negative impact on a person's life when they have social anxiety disorder. [12]

Social anxiety can have a significant impact on a person's day-to-day activities and routines, which can ultimately lead to social isolation. Social stress can cause tension in relationships. Both social stress and social anxiety are responses to emotions, but social stress is often brought on by an outside stimulus. On the other hand, social anxiety is characterized by recurrent and excessive anxieties that do not disappear even when there is no stressor present. Social stress can be a threat to one's connections, esteem, or sense of belonging between two people, within a group, or in a larger social environment. Although social stress is not as severe as social anxiety, it can have a similar effect. For instance, this feeling may be the result of challenging social interactions, such as a stormy marriage or a strained relationship with a member of one's family. [13]

Stress and younger generations

Young people in Australia face a significant risk to their health from the effects of stress. According to a Mission Australia study done in 2015, nearly 40% of young people aged 15 to 19 are extremely concerned about their ability to deal with stress.

Teenagers' lives are typically filled with a healthy dose of stress, which can be triggered by a wide variety of factors. The more we understand about how stress affects adolescents, the more equipped we will be as parents to demonstrate the kinds of actions that can teach our children how to deal with stress in healthier ways. The ability to recognize the causes of stress and develop strategies for more effective stress management is a valuable life skill.

Common Stressors in the Lives of Teens

Stress is something that affects every kid to some degree; nevertheless, many adolescents suffer from high levels of stress that are comparable to those of adults. Think about whether any of these probable sources of stress in teenagers are impacting you.

The Stress in America Survey (2017) conducted by the American Psychological Association found that the levels of stress experienced by teenagers are comparable to those experienced by adults. The findings of the poll indicate that not only do adolescents recognize that they are experiencing unhealthy levels of stress, but they also grossly underestimate the impact that stress has on both their mental and physical health.

School is cited as the leading source of stress for adolescents (83 percent), followed by worries about getting into a good college or determining what to do after high school (69 percent), and then worries about their family's financial situation (63 percent) (65 percent).

In the past month, a significant number of adolescents have reported that stress caused them to lie awake at night (35 percent), overeat or consume unhealthy foods (26 percent), and skip meals (23 percent).

Because of stress, in the previous month, forty percent of adolescents have reported feeling irritable or angry, thirty-six percent have reported feeling worried or anxious, thirty-six percent have reported feeling lethargic or tired, and thirty-one percent have reported feeling overwhelmed.

When asked, more than one-quarter of adolescents (26 percent) admitted that they had yelled at or been short with classmates or teammates in the past month when they were upset. At least once a month, someone comments to at least fifty-one percent of adolescents that they appear to be stressed.

On a scale of one to ten, the average degree of stress that adolescents report having throughout the school year is 5.8 points, however during the summer, this number drops to 4.6 points.

Warning Signs for Stress

Every adolescent goes through at least a little bit of stress, and a certain amount of it is actually good for them. However, a large number of adolescents battle with high levels of stress, which can inhibit their ability to study, their ability to form healthy relationships, and their performance in other aspects of their lives. Many diverse manifestations of stress are possible, and some of the symptoms of stress are similar to behaviors that are typical of teenagers. Teens are particularly susceptible to developing stress because of this. When it comes to the signs of stress in teenagers, it is essential to be aware of what to look for:

Alterations in mood: you may notice that your adolescent is becoming more irritable, worried, or depressed. Observe any shifts in behavior and take note of them.

Traumatic bodily changes: Stressed-out teenagers tend to get sick and report of bodily discomforts such as tension headaches, nausea, and sore muscles.

Changes in behavior: Be on the lookout for alterations in eating or sleeping patterns, as well as an avoidance of typical day-to-day activities.

Changes in cognition may include a diminished ability to concentrate, increased forgetfulness, and/or an outward manifestation of carelessness.

Common Stressors in the Lives of Teens

Every adolescent is unique, and there are many various things that can cause them to feel stressed out. The findings of the survey entitled "Stress in America" indicate that there are a few frequent causes of stress among the nation's teenage population. Communicating about stress in an open and forthright manner with your adolescent is the most effective method to gain insight into how your child copes with stress and the causes of that stress. It is essential for parents to destigmatize the experience of stress in their children and encourage their adolescents to develop healthy coping mechanisms.

Take into account the following potential sources of stress for teenagers:

The Pressure of Schoolwork

Teenagers suffer significant amounts of stress associated to school on a variety of levels, including grades, test scores, and the process of applying to colleges. Many adolescents experience anxiety because they are concerned about meeting the academic obligations placed on them, satisfying their instructors and parents, and keeping up with their classmates. The inability to effectively manage one's time or the experience of being overpowered by one's workload are both factors that might contribute to academic stress.

Pressure from Society

Teenagers lay a significant emphasis on their relationships with their peers. In their day-to-day lives, they spend a large portion of their time with their peers, making it harder to find and sustain a tribe. Adolescents face a variety of stressors, including bullying and other subtle types of relational violence, but gaining the skills to deal with healthy disagreement and navigate romantic relationships is no small feat. Bullying and other subtle forms of relational aggression are clear sources of stress for adolescents. When a person is a teenager, one of the additional stresses they face is that of peer pressure. Teens may participate in conduct that is beyond of their comfort zones in order to placate their classmates. This may be done in an effort to create and keep friendships with their peers.

Discord within the family

Everything that happens in the home might have an effect on the adolescent since stress is a domino effect. Unrealistic expectations, trouble in the marriage, poor relationships with siblings (including bullying by siblings), illness within the family, and financial hardship on the family can all contribute to an increase in the level of stress experienced by teenagers.

What's Going On in the World

In addition to causing stress for teenagers, events such as gun violence, terror attacks, and natural disasters can also worry their parents. Many teens have access to 24-hour news coverage, which might lead them to worry about themselves and their loved ones' safety when they hear terrible stories from both domestic and international sources on a daily basis.

Traumatic Events

Adversities such as the passing of a family member or close friend, an accident, illness, or the continuation of emotional or physical abuse can have a long-lasting effect on the levels of stress experienced by teenagers. It's also essential to keep in mind that roughly 10 percent of young people experience violence in their romantic relationships.

Significant Shifts in One's Life

Significant life transitions can cause stress for adolescents, just as they can for adults. Moving to a new location, beginning attendance at a new school, or experiencing changes in the composition of the family (such as divorce or the formation of mixed families) are all potential stressors for adolescents. For a maturing adolescent, not being aware of how to deal with significant life events can be stressful and lead to confusion.

Teenage girls are the demographic most likely to be influenced by the social stress that is the most prevalent of these stressors, and this form of stressor is the one that has the greatest influence. Social Stress can be caused by a number of different parts of society; however, the social media are by far the most significant contributor to the social stress experienced by young girls.

Teenagers' Mental Health Is Affected by Social Media

The fact that today's kids face a very real issue in the form of the demand to be present on social media at all times should not come as a surprise to anyone. Not only do kids have a far better understanding of and dependence on social media than many adults do, but they also use it at considerably higher rates than adults do. This is in addition to the fact that they are much more dependent on it.

According to research conducted by Common Sense Media, over 75 percent of adolescents in the United States have social media profiles. The great majority of adolescents regularly engage in activities related to social media. [14]

The Adolescent Brain and Its Relation to Social Media

Many preteens and teenagers experience something close to addiction when they use social media. Researchers at the UCLA brain mapping center conducted a study in which they discovered that particular parts of the brains of teenagers got engaged when they received "likes" on social media, which in some cases caused them to want to use social media more. [15]

In the course of the research, an fMRI scanner was utilized to take pictures of the brains of 32 adolescents as they used a made-up version of Instagram to simulate a social networking app. The adolescents were presented with more than 140 pictures that had "likes" that were presumed to be from their contemporaries. On the other hand, the research team was the one who really selected the likes. [15]

As a consequence of this, the brain scans revealed that in addition to a number of locations, the nucleus accumbens, which is part of the brain's reward circuitry, was notably active when the individuals observed a big number of likes on their own images. According to the findings of several studies, this part of the brain is the same one that lights up when we see photographs of the people we care about or when we get a financial windfall.

Researchers have shown that the area of the brain responsible for processing rewards is especially responsive in adolescents, which may help to explain why adolescents are so drawn to social networking platforms. [15]

Social media and peer influence were linked in a distinct area of the study, the researchers discovered. Participants were exposed to both safe and harmful images as part of the study.

Participants in the study showed no effect of image category on how many "likes" were given to photos.

Instead, they were more likely to click the "like" button on popular photographs, despite the content of the photos they liked. According to the results of this study, experts believe that peers can have both a positive and harmful impact on others while accessing social media. [15]

The state of one's mind

There is no doubt that the use of social networking sites plays a significant part in both the expansion of teens' social connections and the development of their valuable technological abilities. But what kind of mental toll does participating in all of this social networking take on adolescents and young adults? According to the majority of reports, the impact may be rather significant. [16]

Not only does spending so much time online put growing brains at risk, but adolescents frequently struggle to self-regulate the amount of time they spend in front of screens, thus the more time they spend in front of a computer, the greater the potential for problems. In addition, they are more likely to give in to peer pressure, engage in cyberbullying, or send sexually explicit messages (all activities that include digital communication), which might make it difficult for them to navigate the social world of the internet. [16]

Depression

Researchers are just starting to establish a connection between mental health issues and the use of social media. Social media use has been linked to an increase in depression symptoms, such as a decrease in social interaction and an elevation in feelings of isolation, despite the lack of proof of a cause-and-effect link between depression and social media use. [17]

For example, a study that was recently published in the journal Computers in Human Behavior discovered that the usage of several social media sites is a more significant factor in the development of depression than the total amount of time spent online. According to the findings of the study, the risk of depression was more than three times as high among participants who used more than seven social media platforms as it was among participants who used two or fewer sites. [18]

There have been a number of new studies that have pointed to the possibility that prolonged use of social media may be related to the signs and symptoms of mental health conditions such as depression, anxiety, and low self-esteem, particularly in children. [18]

Anxiety

Many times, adolescents experience strong feelings of emotional investment in their social media profiles. They not only feel the need to respond fast online, but also the pressure to have flawless images and articles that are well written, all of which can generate a tremendous deal of worry for them. In point of fact, a number of studies have discovered that the greater a teen's social circle is online, the higher their level of anxiety is regarding their ability to keep up with everything that is happening online.

To remain current with the unstated norms and customs of each social media site requires a significant investment of both time and effort. As a consequence of this, more pressure is placed on teenagers, which can lead to feelings of anxiousness in some cases.

In addition, if adolescents make a social faux pas online, this can be an extremely stressful situation for them. Many adolescents, particularly young women, have a tendency to worry about what other people may be thinking about them and how they will react the next time they encounter them. When you add in instances of cyberbullying, slut-shaming, and other harsh online behaviors, it is easy to understand why many adolescents find social media to be a toxic source of worry. [18]

Sleep Deprivation

An increasing number of teenagers are unable to get enough sleep because of their overreliance on social media. Due to these and other side effects, sleep deprivation can lead to irritation, lower grades, decreased drive for physical exercise, and overeating. It can also worsen preexisting issues such as depression, anxiety and ADHD. [17]

In point of fact, research has shown a substantial connection between increasing screen usage and the development of ADHD-related symptoms. These symptoms include difficulties focusing, problems regulating emotions, poor concentration, hyperactivity, and not getting enough sleep. [19]

In addition, a study that was conducted in Britain and published in the Journal of Youth Studies questioned 900 adolescents between the ages of 12 and 15 about their usage of social media and how it affected their quality of sleep. What they discovered was that one in five of the adolescents admitted that they "nearly usually" wake up in the middle of the night to check their social media accounts.

In addition, the survey found that girls were substantially more likely than boys to get up and check social media on their phones first thing in the morning. In addition to expressing that they were exhausted all the time, they also stated that they were generally less pleased than teenagers whose sleep was not disrupted by social media. [20]

In addition, adolescents have a higher minimum sleep requirement than adults do, which ranges from eight to ten hours each night as opposed to seven or more for adults. Therefore, logging into social media at an inappropriate time, such as the middle of the night, can be harmful to a person's physical health. For instance, in addition to making a person feel weary and angry, not getting enough sleep can increase the risk of getting into an accident, decrease the immune system, and make it more difficult for teens to fight off diseases. [21]

Envy

Jealousy and envy are natural feelings, but they may wreak havoc on the brains of adolescents if they constantly compare themselves to others in their peer group. It's possible for individuals to become obsessed with something that another person possesses or has experienced but they themselves have not. The manner in which tales are curated can give the impression to the reader that other people's lives are more interesting than their own, which only serves to reinforce feelings of inadequacy. [22]

Teenagers, however, do not often comprehend that individuals prefer to simply share their "highlight reel" on social media and frequently keep the mundane or tough experiences off of the Internet. This is something that kids often do not realize. Because of this, the life of another person may appear to be picture perfect online, but in real life, they face challenges just like everyone else.

In spite of this, it is very simple for an adolescent to fall into the comparison trap and begin to believe that everyone else has it better or is happy than they are. As a consequence of this, it is possible for this to feed into feelings of melancholy, loneliness, rage, and a range of other problems.

In addition, if it is not handled with, envy can sometimes escalate to bullying and other forms of negative conduct. Some adolescents, particularly those who have low self-esteem, pick on other adolescents because they are envious of the victim's appearance, whether it be their clothes, their body, their lover, their triumphs, or any number of other things. [23]

Communication Issues

Even though communicating with friends and family via social media is a fantastic method to stay in touch with them, it is important to remember that it cannot replace in-person interaction. For instance, an adolescent cannot see the facial emotions of another person online nor can they hear the tone of their speech. As a consequence of this, it is incredibly simple for individuals to misunderstand one another, particularly when they are attempting to be humorous or caustic online.

There are a lot of teenagers who spend so much time checking their statuses and getting "likes" on social media sites that they forget to talk to the individuals who are standing right in front of them. When a person's life revolves almost entirely around social media, it's not uncommon for their friendships and dating relationships to suffer as a result. As a consequence of this, adolescents run the risk of having connections that are neither profound nor genuine.

Teens who place an emphasis on social media are more likely to concentrate on taking images that demonstrate how much fun they are having rather than truly concentrating on the experience of having fun itself. As a consequence, the quality of their relationships and overall life satisfaction may decline as a consequence.

How to Deal with the Stress of Social Situations

However, social media and messaging applications, which allow for such immediate and spontaneous emotions as well as emotional expressions depending on those reactions, might make it even more challenging for adolescent girls to navigate their social lives. It can be challenging for parents to determine the most effective strategy to assist their teenage daughters in coping with the pressures of social situations.

It is essential to keep in mind that the brains of teenagers are not fully matured, and that during this stage of life, extremely significant changes and developments take place in the brain. When it comes to logical reasoning, the prefrontal cortex of the brain is the most important area of our brain. It is common for teenagers to be affected by the limbic portion of their brains, which is linked to emotions, responsiveness, and impulsivity, and is often a natural propensity. The limbic system is linked to this part of the brain.

In order for parents to be in a position to be strategic and effective in assisting their teenage daughters in navigating the challenges of social stress, it will be extremely helpful for them to have an understanding of what is happening during the process of brain development in adolescents.

Make an effort to get rid of the sources of stress

The severity of the circumstance, in addition to the person who is going through it, is a factor in determining whether or not an individual may experience an unacceptable amount of psychological stress. The way in which you understand and think about a stressful situation can also have a significant influence on how you react to it. You may not always be able to get out of a stressful situation or sidestep a problem, but you can make an effort to lower the amount of stress that you are experiencing. Consider whether the circumstances that are causing you stress may be altered in any way, such as by relinquishing part of your responsibilities, lowering your expectations, or seeking assistance from others.

Cultivate social support

Strong social support can boost resilience to stress. Make an effort to connect with others. It's possible that some of your close friends or family members are excellent listeners and can empathize with you. Some people are more skilled than others at providing hands-on assistance, such as bringing a home-cooked meal or watching children for an hour. The act of supporting others can also boost pleasant feelings and reduce the intensity of negative ones. Just remember to keep a healthy equilibrium in your interactions. Your level of stress may be raised if you have a friend who always needs help but never gives it.

Seek out healthy ways of eating

In response to the presence of a stressor, the central nervous system secretes adrenaline and cortisol, which, among other physiological repercussions, have an effect on the gastrointestinal tract. Acute stress can produce loss of appetite, but prolonged stress can cause desires for sweet and fatty foods because of the hormone cortisol that is released during that state. A high amount of cortisol, in combined with a high sugar diet, has been shown to promote the deposition of fat around the internal organs. The accumulation of fat in the abdominal cavity has been related to an increased risk of cardiovascular and metabolic diseases. A well-balanced diet that includes a wide variety of nutrients can both safeguard one's health and offer the energy needed to overcome problems. Giving up sweets or going vegan isn't necessary; instead, aim to include more colored vegetables and fruits on a daily basis. It is important to refrain from using substances such as alcohol to mitigate the impacts of stress because doing so will not address the underlying cause of the issue and may have adverse repercussions on your health.

Relax your muscles

Because stress causes muscles to stiffen up, being stressed out can induce tension headaches, backaches, and overall weariness in addition to the specific aches and pains. Stretching, massage, and taking warm baths are all effective ways to combat stress and the symptoms it causes. Alternately, you might attempt progressive muscle relaxation, a technique that has been demonstrated to lessen feelings of anxiety and enhance general mental health. In order to do progressive muscle relaxation, you must first find a position that is comfortable and then select a muscle group to relax, such as the muscles in your calf muscles. After drawing in your breath and tensing your muscles for anywhere from five to ten seconds, quickly let out your breath and relax them. After relaxing for at least ten seconds, proceed to the next muscle group in the body. The technique of passive progressive muscle relaxation is still another choice. This method is quite similar to progressive muscle relaxation, except instead of beginning with tensing the muscles, it goes straight into relaxing them. Imagine each muscle group separately, one at a time, and concentrate your efforts on unwinding the associated section of your body.

Meditate

There is a growing body of evidence suggesting that mindful meditation can alleviate the psychological tension and anxiety that people experience; even mindfulness meditation programs that are only a few weeks long are effective. To get started, find a calm spot where you can sit down for five minutes and focus on deep breathing. Keep your attention fixed on the here and now; if distracting thoughts pop into your head, simply acknowledge them and then let them go. Don't be so hard on yourself if you find your mind wandering. Redirect the attention in a calm manner so that it is brought back to the here and now.

Be sure to guard your rest

The effects of stress during the day might be felt during sleep. To make matters even more difficult, lack of sleep can have an impact on both one's mental state and their emotions. How to sleep better? Make an effort to establish a regular bedtime routine that includes some downtime before you turn the lights off. Sleeplessness can benefit from practices like meditation and relaxation. Additionally, stay away from caffeinated beverages and alcoholic beverages in the late afternoon and evening. Put away your screens, because blue light can prevent the production of the hormone melatonin, which helps us sleep (and checking social media may ramp up your emotions.)

Finally, make sure you keep moving throughout the day: A significant body of evidence indicates that engaging in physical activity can enhance sleep quality, particularly for persons of middle age and older.

Do something active

Not only can brisk movement help enhance sleep quality, but it can also directly battle the negative effects of stress. According to the findings of one study, working adults who participated in moderate levels of physical activity reported significantly lower levels of stress compared to working adults who did not participate. The detrimental consequences of stress, such as its influence on the immune system, may be mitigated or even eliminated entirely by engaging in physical activity, according to some studies. Increasing your level of physical activity doesn't have to be complicated or expensive; all it takes is a brisk 30-minute stroll or some dancing in the living room to achieve the desired results.

Take a break to enjoy the outdoors

Studies carried out in a variety of nations have come to the conclusion that exposure to green space improves one's mood. Even videos of nature have been shown to hasten recovery from stress, particularly when compared to videos of metropolitan settings. Bringing your attention to the natural world around you, even in the shape of a crowded urban park, can help you refocus and relax your thoughts.

Don't give up on the things that make you happy

When people's lives become too stressful, they frequently cut back first on their leisure pursuits. However, denying oneself all forms of pleasure may not be in your best interest. Even when time is limited, it is important to look for opportunities to do something for yourself. This could include things like reading a book, singing along to your favorite songs, or watching your favorite comedy on Netflix. The mental and physical health of an individual can both benefit from humor and laughter. Transform your way of thinking: Cognitive behavioral therapy, sometimes known as CBT, is one of the therapies for stress and anxiety that has the most backing from scientific study. This kind of psychotherapy is predicated on the realization that our thoughts have an effect on our feelings, which in turn has a bearing on the actions that we take. It is possible to better control your emotions and, as a result, experience less stress by changing the way you think about the things that are stressful to you. A few pointers: If you find yourself beginning to imagine the worst possible outcomes, you should immediately stop and redirect your thoughts to something else. Establish reasonable goals and standards for yourself. Make an effort to accept the things that are happening that you can't change.

Seek help

Find a psychologist or another mental health specialist who can teach you how to successfully manage your stress if you are having trouble dealing with it on your own and you are not getting any relief from trying to help yourself. They will be able to assist you in determining the circumstances or actions that are contributing to your stress, after which they will assist you in developing a strategy to change the stressors, modify your surroundings, and change your responses.

Advice for the Mothers and Fathers

In order to maintain good mental health and wellbeing during the preteen and teenage years, stress management is essential. Your youngster can learn how to better manage their stress with your assistance.

Recognize the strain that your youngster is under

Tell your child that you have seen that they are stressed and that you are available to help them if you notice that they are stressed. Your ability to respond to your child with warmth and compassion can assist them in being more compassionate toward themselves. It is possible for adolescents to alleviate the negative effects of stress and assist your child in "bouncing back" during or after trying moments if they practice self-compassion and treat themselves with kindness.

Determine the factors that are contributing to the stress

It may be simpler for your child to cope with the stress if they are aware of the factors that are contributing to it. You can be of assistance by requesting that your child record all of the activities that they are participating in on paper. After then, students are able to contemplate how they feel about these issues. For instance, does your child find that some of them cause them to feel tight or prevent them from sleeping?

Keep in mind that pleasant experiences can also be difficult, and that having an excessive amount of work can also cause stress.

Figure out how to deal with things that are stressful

You might begin by assisting your child in developing a hierarchy of priorities for which tasks require immediate attention and which can wait. There are ways to alleviate some of the tension. For instance, if your child has stress due to the fact that they are frequently late for school in the morning, they may be able to alleviate some of that tension by preparing themselves the night before or rising earlier.

There are some stressful events for which preparation is possible. For instance, if your child is extremely anxious about an approaching test, you might assist them in getting ready by developing a study schedule with them as a group.

There are some things that cause stress that can't be altered, but such things can be discussed. For instance, if your child is stressed about the financial position of your family, listening to their concerns and having a conversation with them about those issues could help to minimize the amount of stress they feel.

Encourage a lifestyle that is good for your health

Making healthy lifestyle choices can frequently assist your child in coping with stress or lessening its consequences. The following are some suggestions for your kid:

Get some exercise and stay active

Your child's mood can benefit from physical activity and exercise, and they can also gain a sense of accomplishment in addition to having their physical health improved. Cortisol, popularly known as the "stress hormone," can be burned off by exercise, which in turn can help the body relax.

Eat healthy and delicious cuisine

A healthy diet can assist your child in feeling good, being strong, having lots of energy, being attentive, and being able to concentrate.

Take some time to unwind and relax, especially before going to bed

This could involve going for a stroll, reading a book, taking a soothing bath, listening to music, or engaging in activities such as breathing exercises, muscular relaxation exercises, or mindfulness exercises.

Sleep well

Your preteen or teenager needs approximately 8-10 hours of sleep every night, and if they get the amount of quality sleep they need, it can help them feel more aware, cheerful, and active throughout the day. One of the most significant contributors to stress in adolescents is an insufficient amount of sleep.

Stay away from narcotics of any kind, including coffee, alcohol, and other substances

Although older teenagers and adults frequently use alcohol and other substances to cope with stress, research has shown that these substances actually make stress symptoms worse and can lead to additional problems.

9. Kill the Panic Attacks

Anxiety and terror are accompanied by bodily symptoms such a racing heart, rapid breathing, and perspiration in panic attacks. Panic disorder, a form of anxiety illness, can develop as a result of these attacks. Anxiety episodes can be prevented with therapy and anti-anxiety medication.

Panic attacks are what they sound like

A panic episode is distinguished by its suddenness and severe, immobilizing severity. If you're having a panic attack, your heart is racing, you're having trouble breathing, and you may fear you're going insane or about to die. Without warning or a clear trigger, some panic attacks can occur out of the blue. Even when you're comfortable or sleepy, they can still happen.

Despite the fact that panic attacks can recur again, the majority of people only suffer from one attack. Repeat panic attacks can be caused by a specific situation, such crossing a street or giving a public speech, particularly if it has happened before. To activate the body's fight or flight reaction, a panic-inducing circumstance is usually one where you feel threatened and have no way out.

Even if you have a panic episode or two, you'll still be fine and healthy otherwise. If you have panic disorder, social phobia, or depression, your panic episodes could be a symptom of these disorders. No matter what causes them, panic episodes can be managed. There are ways to reduce or eliminate panic symptoms, reclaim your self-confidence, and regain control of your life.

Are panic attacks common?

Anxiety attacks affect up to 11% of the population in the United States each year. Panic disorder affects 2% to 3% of people with the condition.

Causes of Panic Attacks

Having a panic attack is something that can happen to everyone. Among the contributing elements are the following:

Panic episodes usually begin in adolescence or the early years of adulthood for most people. Panic episodes, however, can strike anyone of any age, including youngsters.

Panic disorder is twice as common in women as it is in males.

Panic attacks are triggered by what?

It is not completely understood why certain people are susceptible to panic episodes or why they develop panic disorder. The nervous system and the brain both play important roles in how you react to and deal with stressful situations. Panic attacks are more likely if you have any of the following:

There is a strong genetic link between anxiety disorders, such as panic disorders, and their prevalence in families. No one knows why.

Panic attacks are more common in those with mental health concerns, such as anxiety disorders, depression, or any other type of mental illness.

A person's vulnerability to panic attacks can be exacerbated if they are abusing alcohol or other drugs.

A heart attack or panic attack

Panic attacks are often so severe that people assume they're experiencing a heart attack as a result of their physical symptoms. However, a large number of patients are forced to seek medical attention because they fear they have a life-threatening medical condition that requires immediate attention. Symptoms like chest pain, a raised heart rate, or difficulty breathing should always be thoroughly investigated to rule out medical explanations. However, panic is often neglected as a probable cause, not the other way around.

Symptoms of a Panic attack

The symptoms of a panic attack usually peak within ten minutes of their onset. Their average duration is 20-30 minutes and they rarely last longer than an hour. Panic attacks can strike anybody, at any moment, and without warning. Shopping, going down the street or resting on your couch at home might all trigger an attack of the flu-like symptoms.

Indications of a panic attack include:
- Hyperventilation or shortness of breath
- Having a beating heart or palpitations
- Chest discomfort or pain
- Shaking or trembling
- Suffocating sensation - a sense of disconnection from one's immediate environment
- Sweating
- a feeling of sickness or discomfort in the stomach
- having a feeling of faintness

- Feelings of numbness or tingling are common symptoms.
- Flashes of heat or cold
- A phobia of death, loss of control, or psychosis

Anxiety-like symptoms can also be caused by serious medical conditions such as heart disease, thyroid illness, and respiratory difficulties. It is possible that your doctor will order testing to rule out a physical condition. There may be a diagnosis made based on your symptoms and risk factors when there is no physical cause.

Panic disorder can be diagnosed in a variety of ways

Panic disorder can be diagnosed by a doctor or therapist. When you have recurrent panic attacks with the following symptoms, your healthcare professional may diagnose panic disorder.

Panic attacks and their repercussions are a constant source of anxiety for me.

During a panic attack, worry excessively about losing control. Take precautions to prevent yourself from experiencing a panic attack.

What are the long-term effects of panic episodes on the body?

Anxiety episodes can be successfully treated. Sadly, many people put off getting help because they're ashamed. Panic disorders and panic attacks, if left untreated, can make it difficult to enjoy the little things in life. It's possible that you'll:

Anxiety induced by the prospect of a panic episode is known as anticipatory anxiety.

Phobias: An intense and unjustified fear of a single thing is what is meant by the term "phobia." Acrobatic fear is related to the fear of heights, as is claustrophobia, which has to do with the fear of small spaces.

People with panic disorder are twice as likely to develop agoraphobia as the general population as a whole. This anxiety disorder causes you to avoid places and situations where a panic attack could occur. The terror can get so bad that you won't leave the house.

Panic disorder signs and symptoms

One or two panic attacks may be all it takes for some people to develop panic disorder, but it's not something to be concerned about for those who have just had one or two panic attacks. The hallmarks of panic disorder are recurrent panic episodes, significant alterations in behavior, or a persistent fear of experiencing another attack.

Panic disorder may be present if you:

Think about another panic attack all the time

Because of the panic attacks, you've changed your behavior, such as avoiding situations where you've panicked before.

Despite the fact that a panic episode often lasts only a few minutes, its lingering repercussions can be felt for years to come. When you suffer from panic disorder, the recurrence of panic attacks has a significant psychological impact. Because of the trauma you experienced during the assaults, your self-esteem may suffer, and your daily routine may be severely disrupted. When this happens, it eventually results in the following symptoms of panic disorder:

Between panic attacks, you should feel calm and collected. Instead, you're tense and apprehensive. This is called anticipatory anxiety. Anxiety is a result of dread of having another panic attack in the near future. This "fear of terror" is all too common and can be crippling for those who experience it.

Certain situations or environments cause you to become phobic, therefore you begin to avoid them. Avoidance may be motivated by a fear of re-experiencing a panic episode that was sparked by a similar event. Another option is to stay away from situations where it would be difficult to get out if you had a panic attack or where aid would be unavailable. Phobic avoidance becomes agoraphobia when taken to its logical conclusion.

Anxiety and agoraphobia are symptoms of panic disorder

The old understanding of agoraphobia was that it manifested as a fear of open settings, such as public venues. It is now widely accepted that agoraphobia is a result of panic attacks and panic disorder, rather than the other way around. In the first year following the onset of recurrent panic attacks, you are more likely to acquire agoraphobia than at any other time in that year.

An agoraphobic is terrified of having a panic attack in a scenario where it would be difficult or embarrassing to get out of the circumstance. Having a panic attack and not being able to get treatment is another possibility. You avoid more and more situations as a result of your anxieties.

Start by avoiding, for example:

Crowded locations like shopping malls and sports stadiums, cars, planes, subways, and other modes of transportation. Panic attacks should be avoided in public places such as bars and restaurants.

In the event that physical activity causes a panic attack. Alcohol, caffeine, sugar, and some drugs can all cause panic attacks.

Leaving the house without someone to keep you company and give you a sense of security. You may only feel comfortable at home in the most extreme instances.

Anxiety disorders and panic attacks: possible causes

In spite of the fact that the actual origins of panic attacks and panic disorder remain a mystery, there is a strong familial link. Major life events such as graduating from college, getting married, or having a baby tend to be linked to depression. The death of a loved one, a divorce, or a job loss can also lead to panic attacks that are triggered by severe stress.

Medical disorders and other physical factors might also contribute to panic episodes. Doctors can rule out the following options if a person is experiencing panic symptoms:

Mitral valve prolapse, a condition in which one of the heart's valves does not seal properly, is a minor cardiac ailment.

A condition known as hyperthyroidism (overactive thyroid gland)

Diabetic ketoacidosis (low blood sugar)

Addiction to stimulants (amphetamines, cocaine, caffeine)

Withdrawal from narcotics

Panic Attacks: How to "Kill" Them

You're not the only one who suffers from panic attacks in stressful or frightening situations. Even while these episodes are rarely life-threatening, they are frightening nonetheless, and you'll naturally want to avoid them at all costs. There are natural ways to deal with panic attacks in addition to those prescribed by your doctor. You can overcome a panic attack by focusing on your breath and remaining calm. To avoid having more panic attacks in the future, take measures to lessen your worry and stress in your daily life.

How to deal with it

The physical and mental signs of a panic attack can be identified. When you're suffering a panic attack, the physical symptoms are likely to be the first thing you notice. In order to spot a panic attack, you must pay attention to your body and what it is telling you. [24]

Starting with chest tightness, shortness of breath and feeling faint, panic attacks can cause nausea and stomach cramps in addition to sweating and shaking.

In addition, you're likely to have a quick onset of fear and anxiety. As a result, your level of fear may rise because you feel as if you are losing control of yourself or the situation.

Symptoms typically begin to grow in intensity within 10 to 20 minutes of its onset. The panic attack normally reaches its peak at this point.

Having a panic attack for the first time can be really frightening. There are many people who are able to overcome their panic attacks, so don't worry about it!

Acknowledge that you had a panic attack

Identify the source of your anxiety and take steps to reduce it. It's tempting, but resisting or denying the attack will only make it worse. Tell yourself, "I'm experiencing a panic attack," and let it go. Acknowledging the truth may feel like you're giving up, but it's a sensible way to approach the situation. You can get through a panic attack if you keep your awareness up. [25]

If someone is nearby, tell them you're having a panic attack and that you'll need some time to calm down.

Positivity Talk

In order to get through this, you need to tell yourself that everything will be fine. A panic attack's unpleasant feelings can be countered with positive words. Positive self-talk, such as "I'll get through this" or "It will be over soon," can help you stay focused. Do this as long as it takes for you to feel better. [26]

Tell yourself that if this is your first time going through a panic attack, it will get better with practice.

It's also helpful to talk rationally to yourself. "This won't hurt me, and I'll be fine when it's over" is a good way to convince yourself that you aren't in imminent danger.

Avoid hyperventilation by using the 4-7-8 breathing technique

A panic attack can get worse if you hyperventilate or take in a lot of rapid breaths. Breathe in and out slowly and deeply. Inhale deeply through your nose for 4 breaths. Count to 8 while slowly exhaling your breath after holding it in for 7 seconds. As a result, the attack will not get any worse as a result of this. [27]

It's a good idea to make a "whoosh" sound with your lips when you exhale to keep your attention on your breathing and keep the panic attack at bay.

The ability to close your eyes and filter out the rest of the world while you're breathing is also a useful tool.

Stay rooted in the circumstance by focusing on your surroundings

This is a fantastic approach to keep your mind from racing during a panic attack. Look around and identify the sounds, sights, and smells you encounter. Even if they seem insignificant, say them aloud to yourself. You'll be able to distract yourself from the fear eventually.

The birds by the lake, the folks on the bench, the bus passing by, and the smell of the hot dog vendor across the park are all things you'll notice.

While doing this, be sure to maintain a deep inhale

A good way to keep yourself safe is to pay attention to what's going on around you. When this happens, your brain is able to calm down.

With progressive muscle relaxation, you can let go of your stress.

Each muscle group in your body is trained to release and release the tension that occurs with a panic attack with this exercise. If you can, lay down on a flat surface to begin with. Then, before releasing the tension in your facial muscles, squeeze them as firmly as you can. As you make your way down your body, keep doing the same thing. Using this approach on a daily basis can help you relax your body and mind. [28]

When you're having a panic attack, use this approach to help you calm down and relax. It is much easier to execute during an attack if you have practiced.

Muscle relaxation also has beneficial effects on the body's health. If you frequently have aches and pains in your muscles, this technique can help.

Take your mind off of things

Take a break from the panic attack by recalling a good experience or imagining a better future. Changing your thinking from negative to positive can help you get through an assault. Reflect on what makes you laugh or smile. Distract yourself by thinking about something nice.

You can lift your spirits by gazing at photos of your family or pets, if you're at home. The photographs on your phone are available for viewing whenever and wherever you are.

Practicing Self-Control

Breathe slowly and deeply. Reduce your stress levels by practicing deep breathing techniques. Sit or lie on your back in a cool, peaceful location. Close your eyes and take a deep inhalation of air. Initially, hold it for a few seconds before slowly releasing it. For the best effects, do this for 10 to 20 minutes every day. [29]

There are two advantages to improving your breathing. The first benefit is that it helps alleviate your overall stress and anxiety, which may help prevent panic episodes. If you ever find yourself having a panic attack, you'll know how to stop yourself from hyperventilating thanks to this training.

While you're inhaling and exhaling, listening to soothing music or white noise can help you focus.

Do yoga and meditation

Relaxation and stress reduction can be achieved through both of these hobbies. You can do them at home, or you can take a class if you prefer to have some help and coaching. Try to set aside some time in the morning and at night to engage in these peaceful pursuits. Preparing and winding down are made easier by these items.

As far as you are able to, stay away from the things that cause you anxiety

It is possible that you have a specific cause for your panic episodes, such as heights or stressful situations. Identifying and avoiding the problem's trigger is one solution. Cut off the trigger if it's not something you have to deal with on a daily basis and you won't notice any negative effects on your life.

Some people's panic or anxiety is triggered by nothing in particular. If you're still unsure, consider the past few times you experienced a panic attack and the activities you were engaged in just before the attack began to give you some insight. If you see any recurring themes, they may be the root cause of your issue.

An effective protection mechanism is not one that interferes with your daily routine. A therapist or psychologist should be seen if you find yourself avoiding a lot of things and it becomes difficult to work or live on a daily basis.

Relaxing Your Nervous System

Stress can be reduced by exercising consistently. Staying active is a well-known stress-busting strategy. Regular physical activity not only enhances your mood, but it also benefits your overall health. For the best effects, stick to 30 minutes of exercise at least five days a week.

Running, riding, or taking kickboxing classes are the finest ways to relieve stress and tension. Weightlifting, for example, is an excellent form of resistance training. For the same benefits, you don't have to work out as hard. A daily walk can do wonders for relieving stress. Make your workouts more pleasurable by including fun hobbies. Go on more hikes if you enjoy the outdoors.

To avoid a dip in blood sugar, eat at regular intervals. When you're hungry, your attitude can take a turn for the worse and you're more prone to panic episodes. Eat regularly and avoid becoming overly hungry to keep your blood sugar levels in check. In between meals, have a little snack.

Never go a day without eating. This results in a low blood sugar collapse, which is depressing to the soul. Fresh food is best, so eat plenty of it. There isn't much evidence to back this up, but some studies suggest that a balanced diet may help reduce stress and anxiety. If you're constantly on the go, it's a good idea to bring a few snacks with you. Keep your energy levels up by snacking on some dried fruit or almonds.

Every night, get at least eight hours of sleep

Lack of sleep also lowers your mood, so make it a priority to get enough sleep each night. The ideal amount of sleep is 8 hours, but the most essential thing is to stick to a regular routine and get some shut-eye. Reading or listening to soothing music before bedtime might help you wind down and prepare you for sleep. Getting out of bed and doing something calming can help you catch some shut-eye if you can't get to sleep.

Before going to bed, turn off all electronic devices. To help you get out of bed in the morning, you may want to turn on the light. Consult your physician if you are a frequent sufferer of sleep deprivation.

Reduce your caffeine consumption in order to alleviate stress.

Your heart rate rises as a result of caffeine. Anxiety and panic attacks can result as a result of this. In addition, it makes it more difficult to fall asleep at night. Caffeinated drinks should be limited to no more than one or two servings per day. [30]

Instead of caffeinated beverages, you might want to experiment with decaffeinated versions. Caffeine may cause a reaction in some people, so it's best to avoid it altogether if you're one of them. Coffee isn't the only stimulant out there. Nicotine and energy drinks have a similar effect on the body.

Try a few herbal remedies to relax you

Only a few plants and essential oils have been scientifically shown to alleviate anxiety. Reduce your anxiety by using treatments that have been evaluated and recommended by specialists. Before using herbal supplements, always check with your doctor to make sure they won't conflict with any prescriptions you're already taking.

Lavender, chamomile, valerian root, and passionflower are among the herbal remedies that may be useful in this situation. You can take these substances every day in the form of supplements or teas. Use these products just as indicated and don't exceed the recommended dosage. Anxiety-relieving kahva was long widely accepted, but new research shows that it can cause liver damage. Stay away from it.

Don't use drugs, don't smoke, and don't drink too much

While these drugs may temporarily alleviate your symptoms, they can also heighten your anxiety and increase your vulnerability to panic attacks. Drink no more than one or two drinks every day, and avoid all illegal narcotics. Avoid smoking as well, as nicotine is a stimulant.

Panic episodes can be triggered by some drugs, particularly hallucinogens. [31] Drinking or taking drugs as a way to deal with your worry might lead to an addiction. For help stopping smoking, consult your doctor.

Seeking Help from a Doctor

Check with your doctor to see if there are any other possibilities. In some situations, symptoms of a panic attack may be linked to a medical condition. A rapid heartbeat, shortness of breath, and pain in the chest call for immediate attention. Make an appointment with your health care physician if you're experiencing panic attack symptoms. As a result, you'll be able to get the best possible treatment for your specific situation.

Diagnosis and treatment will be discussed with you by the doctor. After that, they'll make a diagnosis and go over your treatment choices with you. Treating panic attacks using natural means should be discussed with your doctor. They might be able to provide you some advice in this regard.

Get medical advice on coping with your panic attacks

Panic attacks aren't hazardous, so don't worry about them. However, if they happen frequently, they can be extremely upsetting and make it difficult for you to get through the day. Consult your physician to learn what steps you may take to better manage your illness. Do not ignore these warning signs and seek medical attention right away if they occur to you:

- Frightenedness or dread
- Control is lost.
- Intense heartbeat
- Shivering, shivering, and sweating all over my body.
- breathing difficulties or constriction in the throat
- Pain in the chest
- Involuntary bodily reactions - diarrhea or stomach cramps
- Feeling faint, lightheaded, or dizzy
- Tingling or numbness
- A sense of distance

If panic episodes are interfering with your daily life, you should see a therapist

A therapist is always the best option if you're having panic attacks, but if they're making it difficult for you to get through the day or maintain relationships, you need to seek help. Your therapist can teach you new coping strategies for anxiety and panic attacks. In addition, they'll help you control your panic attacks so that they occur less frequently. For panic attacks, look for a therapist who has dealt with the issue before.

For panic attacks, Cognitive Behavioral Therapy (CBT) is a good option. The goal of cognitive behavioral therapy (CBT) for panic attacks is to help you change the way you think about and feel about your panic attacks in order to alleviate your symptoms of anxiety and dread. [32]

If you experience any of the symptoms of a heart attack, get help immediately.

If you frequently experience panic attacks, you don't need to be concerned. However, panic attacks and heart attacks share many of the same symptoms, so if you fear you're suffering a heart attack, you should seek immediate medical attention. Your recovery will be aided by this information.

Chest pain, shortness of breath, and discomfort in the jaw, neck, shoulder, back, or stomach are all symptoms of a heart attack. In the event that you're suffering from a panic attack, you should begin to feel better within 20 to 30 minutes.

Before using any supplements, consult with your doctor

There are herbal supplements that may help alleviate some of the symptoms of anxiety. Common herbs include chamomile,

St. John's Wort, and valerian root. It's safe to take supplements, but they aren't for everyone. It is possible that your supplements could interact with medications you are currently using, exacerbate your medical conditions, or cause an adverse reaction. Talk to your doctor before taking any supplements.

Take the time to tell your doctor about any current medications or supplements you're on. Tell them you're taking vitamins in the hopes of reducing your panic episodes. Additional supplements may be recommended by your doctor.

10. Master the Art of Conversation

Why wouldn't there be an element of art in all that we do? Almost everything is made more tedious when one lacks flair and panache. Why subject yourself to monotony when you may enjoy beautiful works of art?

Whenever it comes to the fine art of conversation, we have all had the experience of meeting someone who appear to have a natural talent for it. They are able to converse with anyone about anything, and they do so with an apparent lack of difficulty. And while it's true that some people are just born with the natural charisma, the rest of us, luckily, have the ability to grow and perfect our communication abilities.

It is of the utmost importance to have strong communication skills in order to effectively transmit one's thoughts and ideas in order to achieve one's goals. The development of strong conversational skills can be aided by following many of the same recommendations.

Conversation is a sort of communication; yet, it is typically more impromptu and less formal than other forms of communication. We come into talks with the intention of having a nice engagement with the other party in order to meet new people, acquire new knowledge, and have enjoyable social interactions. Chats can range from pleasant debates and witty banter to cerebral conversations and information exchanges. There is a wide range of possibilities when it comes to the types of conversations that might take place.

Being more gregarious, lively, or outgoing isn't necessary for having good conversation skills, but being a comic, dramatic actor, or an excellent storyteller helps.

You might instead cultivate the capacity to listen attentively, ask appropriate questions, and pay attention to the replies, all of which are key traits in the art of conversation. Anyone may enhance their conversational abilities as long as they put in the necessary amount of effort and pay attention to the advice they receive.

The significance of having strong abilities in communication

Learning how to communicate clearly and fluently is one of the most crucial talents one can acquire in their lifetime. Transferring information in order to achieve a greater level of comprehension is what we mean when we talk about communication. Conversations are essential to the growth of language, the trading of thoughts and ideas, and the act of actively listening to one another. People gain knowledge by listening to and observing the mental processes of others, particularly by focusing on facial and bodily expressions.

Conversations with other people in person are the most humanizing and empathetic things we can do. We become better listeners by being fully present with one another. It is in these moments when our capacity for empathy matures. It is the place where we get to experience the joy of being heard and understood by others. Self-reflection, those dialogues we have with ourselves that are the foundation of early growth and continue all throughout life, can be advanced through conversation.

Technology is an integral aspect of modern life; but, because technology has made face-to-face discussion less common in favor of phone conversations, texting, emailing, and other forms of electronic communication, children and young adults have lost crucial skills. In today's society, there is a growing trend away from engaging in dialogue. People of all ages are unable to live without their phones and screens, yet striking a healthy balance is of the utmost importance.

Building Up One's Self-Assurance

Conversation is the most important activity that parents can do to help their children become better language users. My ten grandkids, whose ages range from two months to twelve years, are perfect examples of how dialogue may progress with time. The infant, who is only two months old, grins and coos at me, marking the beginning of an excellent conversation and relationship. While the adults use their imaginations to construct Buzz Lightyear adventures or play word games while swaying endlessly, the three and four year olds communicate with one another by connecting words together to form the beginnings of sentences. As we converse back and forth with one another, they pick up new words and expressions in a way that is very natural to them. The talks of the 5 to 9 year olds take place frequently over face-time because they reside in different locations. Despite this, the chatting still takes place as the children "show and tell" the treasures they discovered and discuss the books that we read together.

When I contact children between the ages of 10 and 12, it might be challenging to have a conversation with them since they are frequently engaged in activities on their mobile devices or other displays, such as playing games or texting. When I am with them, though, all it takes to start a conversation is a simple activity like going for a stroll, riding a bike, or shooting some hoops at the basket. Texting is a technique for 15-year-olds to avoid having to deal with the feelings of others as they enter puberty, which makes social adjustment a challenging process for this age group. They may not have the self-assurance necessary to interact with other people. When dealing with children of any age, the most effective strategy is to enter their world of make believe or to ask them insightful questions that encourage them to explain, describe, or talk about their experiences and interests. Language development and self-assurance in front of an audience are both fostered through engaging in conversation with others.

The link that's been missing all along

A physical link between the two individuals who are actively listening to one another is at the heart of the value of having a face-to-face conversation. When children reach the ages of middle school and higher school, the ability to relate to others is highly influenced by participation in talks, including both listening to and having dialogues with other people. Children are able to experience what it is like to be another person through engaging in conversation. This allows them to better understand and empathize with other people's feelings and perspectives. They have the awareness that other people view and experience things in a different way than they do, which contributes to the growth of empathy and intimacy, as well as laying the foundation for the formation of friendships. It is important to remember that sending or receiving a text message is not the same thing as actually having a conversation with someone. The degree to which one truly understands how a close friend or acquaintance is truly experiencing decreases. Children are able to refrain from being emotionally invested in their expressions of communication because texting allows them the time and space to carefully consider their words before typing them. However, they are missing out on the wealth that comes from conversing with one another, sharing laughter, and learning from one another's failures. It's true that we can't truly connect with one another without exchanging words in person.

A Belief in the Creative Capacity of Humans

Children also require opportunities to conduct discussions with themselves about their thoughts and activities during the day, as well as the ability to play with ideas, reflect on what they did, and develop a sense of ease inside themselves. When toddlers are irritable or restless, giving them time in front of a screen may seem like an easy solution. The most effective solution is to provide them with the opportunity to engage in conversation with their own opinions. We demonstrate a lack of faith in the creative potential of human beings if we fill every spare second of our existence. The ability to learn in school is dependent not only on one's own internal desire but also on one's ability to nurture the seeds of learning that germinate during times of boredom or frustration.

Our sixth graders look forward to going on a camping trip every year in the fall; however, there is one activity known as the "night solo," which requires them to sit alone in the darkness of the woods or a field with nothing but a candle and a journal for one hour. After they got back to their houses, many of the students said that the time they spent by themselves in the dark and under the stars was their favorite part of the experience. Some of the youngsters chose to reflect on their lives by writing in diaries, while others lay on their backs and gazed at the night sky, while still others simply listened to their own internal monologues. It is a gift to the brain to give it time to think and reflect, and it is in this state that intriguing and creative ideas can arise, so it is important that we teach our children to relax and think.

Interactions That Were Designed to Happen

A father discussed the differences in his interactions with his two children, who were 10 years apart in age, as they grew up. He had two children. During the time that he was bathing his first child, he engaged in conversation with the child, played with the child's toys, and imagined alongside the child. Ten years later, when he had his second child, he realized that instead of fully interacting with his child when they were taking a bath, he was only partially engaged with his child while checking his cell phone. He was aware of the shift in dynamic that had occurred in his dealings with his children. Experts recommend striking a balance between the times we spend interacting with our children and the times we spend using electronic devices.

Even if having conversations has become more difficult for all of us as we move more into the realm of technology, there are still ways to start conversations. It is important for families to come to an agreement on when all forms of technology are to be put away so that uninterrupted talks may take place and participation in each other's thoughts can become a top priority. Children of all ages need to have meaningful interactions with give-and-take in order to grow socially, emotionally, and intellectually. The gift of full attention and even just peaceful times together is one that is highly sought after by children, and it is one that parents can provide them.

How to "Master the Art of Conversation"

When we get together with a friend, we always end up sharing the stories of our lives, which can range from the insignificant to the profound. When starting new connections, it's helpful to take part in story-telling exchanges, especially when it comes to sharing secrets. Now, new study is revealing some novel insights on how to get that process started, and how to keep it going – on how to handle conversations in the most effective manner, to transform acquaintances or even total strangers into new buddies, and to turn new friends into lifelong confidantes.

Do talk to strangers

In 2014, two psychologists released what is now considered to be classic research on commuters in Chicago. The study indicated that despite our natural tendency to avoid strangers, we experience greater levels of happiness when we engage in conversation with them. It's important to note that this was accurate for both introverts and extraverts alike. A common misconception among commuters is that strangers don't want to talk to them, which may explain their reluctance to begin up a discussion with someone they don't know. Another discovery was made by the scientists. One of the authors, Nicholas Epley, was part of a team that reported nearly identical results from a study of railway riders in London in 2021. This study was based on data collected from commuters on the London Underground. [31] It should come as no surprise that this phenomenon also affects people in the United Kingdom. Therefore, the next time you find yourself in the company of a stranger, why not attempt striking up a conversation with them? It will most likely go better than you anticipate it will.

However, respect the boundaries of their personal space

Depending on characteristics like gender, culture, context, and familiarity, our preferred private space — the space that we like to maintain between ourselves and whomever we're dealing with — varies from one person to the next. Additionally, the Covid-19 pandemic is having an effect on our preferred personal space. Over 9,000 individuals from 42 countries participated in the 2017 study, which found significant differences between people in cultures like that of South America, the Gulf Region, and Southern Europe and cultures like that of Northern Europe, Asia and North America, wherein people would prefer to stand apart [34]. Therefore, if you don't want to make the person you're talking to feel awkward, it's important to take into consideration the cultural background of the person you're talking to. According to the findings of the research, women in the majority of countries prefer having more space than men do. As the epidemic progressed, the participants' ideal personal distances increased both in reality and online, according to the outcomes of a short research conducted in 2021 in the US. We have grown accustomed to maintaining a greater distance from other individuals. According to this research, with the continued occurrence of Covid-19 infections, we should still want it.

Do dig deep

We know that telling our most personal tales to one another can pave the way for more profound and lasting connections with other people. But how soon after we've met someone should we get past the polite conversation and move on? The response is "straight away" according to a study that was conducted in 2021 and also included Epley and was directed by Michael Kardas. The individuals who took part in this study grossly exaggerated how uncomfortable it would be to have an in-depth chat with a stranger, and they vastly underestimated how intrigued strangers were in hearing their revelations. And despite the fact that the participants had anticipated that they would favor a surface-level talk with a stranger over a more in-depth exchange, this was not the case. They reported feeling closer to one another as a result of the in-depth chats.

Be complimentary to others

Are you concerned that comments such as "Oh, I love your dress!" or "You've got a fantastic sense of humor!" can come across as false or excessively personal, so leading to awkwardness rather than a sense of community with the other person? However, according to the findings of yet another recent study utilizing Epley, which was also published in 2021, you shouldn't. Complimenting someone can bring them closer together, whether they are strangers or friends. Earlier research has shown this to be true. Additionally, there is no expense involved, either monetarily or in terms of the amount of effort required. A study conducted on people in the United States by Xuan Zhao nevertheless revealed that friends underestimated the benefits of receiving compliments from each other, and that they overestimated how awkward it would make them feel to receive a compliment from their friend. This erroneous perspective appeared to have real-world implications, as seen by the fact that the participants generally reported delivering fewer praises than they believed they should give, or even would prefer to give.

What if you don't really believe what you're saying when you give someone a compliment? The researchers believe that people may be reluctant to flatter others with fake comments because they overestimate the possibility that their insincerity will be detected. This could be because generally perceived the probability that their lack of sincerity will be discovered. To put it another way, you should just go ahead and say whatever you want because people are likely to take it at face value anyway.

Don't fret after a talk

One of the most uplifting and heartwarming discoveries that I have ever reported on was the fact that other people like us more than we believe they do. This was the result reached by a study in which complete strangers were linked together for the purpose of having short discussions. After then, participants ranked the degree to which they liked their relationships and the degree to which they believed their partners liked them. And they constantly failed to recognize how much others loved them, despite the fact that they had created a greater first impression than they believed they had. In addition to this, the "liking gap" is larger for people who are more reserved. Therefore, you shouldn't let concerns about how you might have come across to a new friend prevent you from continuing a discussion that you've already started; they're probably more eager to chat again than you might believe they would be.

A study titled "thinking gap" was published in the Journal of Experimental Psychology: General in 2021, and it revealed the existence of yet another gap connected to dialogue [36]. Gus Cooney and his colleagues at the University of Pennsylvania note that after a conversation, people have a tendency to focus on the other person they were speaking with, either by thinking about the stories they shared or the advice they offered.

But despite the fact that we do this ourselves, the team discovered through a series of studies that their participants erroneously believed that they thought more afterwards about a person they'd had a conversation with than the other person did about them. This is despite the fact that we do this ourselves. The group concludes that "together, these investigations suggest that persons remain on the minds of their discussion partners more than they know," and they write this in their conclusion. One of the reasons that this message is so significant is that one of the research found that participants' readiness to reconcile with each other after an argument was altered when they learned how much the other person was truly thinking about them.

Overall, for such a sociable species, we're shockingly lousy at gauging how talks, and the exact substance of these conversations, affect our relationships and our own well-being. This is especially true when it comes to the topic at hand, which is typically a topic of conversation. At the very least, the findings of these research point to a positive conclusion, which is that you should stop worrying and start sharing since everything is better than you believe it is.

Ask Questions

It's true that simply making a statement can be all it takes to kick off a conversation. In most cases, though, you will need some carefully designed questions in order to launch or further a conversation. In order to get to know the other person, display interest, discover common ground, come up with a topic to talk, or find a common ground to discuss, you should ask questions.

This is accomplished more successfully by some queries than by others. For instance, rather than asking closed-ended questions, you should ask open-ended inquiries. A question that is closed-ended can only have one correct response. It's possible that the response will be "yes" or "no," but it might also be a number, a date, or even a person. There is only one correct response, thus this brings an end to the conversation. After that, you will need to consider alternative possibilities in order to get it working again.

A more in-depth response can be given to a question with an open-ended format, which then serves as fodder for the conversation to continue. It is possible to get off to a strong start by asking yourself "who," "what," "when," "where," and "why." In addition, you should rephrase your question in a way that is open to receiving a variety of responses. This provokes thought in other people and reveals that what you really want is dialogue and not information. For instance, the question "What do you do when..." gives the impression that you are looking for a definite answer, whereas the question "What kinds of activities do you do when..." leaves room for a variety of different options.

The collection of information is not the only purpose behind asking questions. You are not conducting an interview with the other individual. The objective here is to connect. Understanding, rapport, and possibly even connections can be formed via the simple act of talking to one another and exchanging ideas, thoughts, and questions with one another.

Take in the Responses

Duh. This seems to be the most obvious next step to me. Why bother asking a question if you have no intention of caring about the answer? However, paying attention requires effort. The majority of us are unable to focus on what the other person is saying because our minds are preoccupied with our own thoughts and conversations. It's possible that you're mentally going through the items on your To Do list, pondering how long it will be until the waiter returns, or simply planning out what you'll say when it's your turn to talk. It is challenging to pay attention to both voices at the same time. Put an end to that mental chatter.

Because we only have one mouth and two ears, we are able to listen to twice as much as we are able to express ourselves verbally. Foster an attitude of inquisitiveness in your thinking. You can learn something from every single person on the earth. Your life will be significantly improved if you are always prepared to hear what others have to say.

However, simply listening is not sufficient on its own. You need to show that you're paying attention to what the other person is saying. Saying "I'm listening" while doing something else is insufficient; this may come as a surprise to you, but it's not good enough. You show that you're paying attention not with words but with your body language and facial expressions. Here are some tips:

Use proper facial expressions. In most cases, this will be a smile. However, if someone is telling you that someone in the family has passed away while you are happy... You have failed to hit the target.

Make sure to make eye contact. However, this is not the case all the time. Staring occurs when a person never takes their gaze away from an object or person. Creepy! When speaking, the majority of individuals make eye contact between 30 and 50 percent of the time, whereas when listening, the majority of people make eye contact between 50 and 70 percent of the time. Aim for roughly fifty percent of the time, and you should be OK.

Maintain a generally still body position. Moving around restlessly is an indication of nervous energy and frequently conveys the message "I want to get out of here." Do not fidget with items, jump around, pick at your clothes, or do anything else distracting. Maintain your composure and focus here and now.

Show that you are aware of the situation. The speaker will know that you are paying attention if you make eye contact and nod or murmur occasionally, as well as if you nod or murmur "Mm-hmm." Listen, and make it clear to the other person that you are doing so.

Respond in relevance to the subject being conversed

An exchange of information and ideas is what is meant to be understood when one speaks about a conversation. It's not simply talking. Or just asking questions. Or just listening. Introverts may at times attempt to avoid conversation by asking questions and allowing the other person to continue talking about themselves. In particular, for people who struggle with social anxiety, this is an excellent initial step to take. However, in order to become proficient in the art of conversation, you must also practice speaking.

As was stated earlier, paying attention is the initial stage in formulating insightful remarks and questions. Occasionally, the conversation will move in a way that you would not anticipate, or it will quickly transition from one topic to another and then another. You were going to offer something amusing or profound, but the topic of discussion has already changed. Let it go.

The second stage is to unwind and calm down. You are carrying about in your head the experiences and information of a whole lifetime's worth of living. Let go of any worries or preconceived notions, and focus on being present and tranquil instead. If you take some deep breaths and let go of any tension, you'll find that the words come to you more easily when you need them. Have faith in yourself.

It is also OK to take a moment during conversations to pause and think. If you are at a loss for words, you could respond with "I've never thought about that before" or "I need to consider that." After then, you should ask another inquiry. Continue to toss the topic of conversation back and forth between the two of you like a lighthearted game of catch. (As a matter of fact, I'm not very good at playing catch. However, it is beneficial to calm down and focus on the task at hand!)

Share

Self-disclosure is often the result of having a meaningful conversation. Give us some background on who you are. And you should encourage others to do the same. It's possible that this will require you to get over your fear of being rejected or your self-consciousness. You are someone who should be known. Your opinion should be taken seriously.

On the other hand, it may mean making it possible for the other person to share in a secure environment. It is possible to foster an environment in which others feel comfortable being themselves and sharing who they are by asking insightful questions, listening carefully to the responses, and responding with respect and tact when necessary.

Self-disclosure doesn't have to be deep. You are not obligated to discuss the most difficult times in your upbringing or the challenges you face in your adult life. You don't have to expose everything just yet. (We beg you, don't!) Just reveal enough information about yourself to show the other individual that you are a real person. Tell a tale, share part of your personal history, and avoid using tired cliches. Give the other individual something they can relate to and build a connection with.

Make sure there is a balance of giving and taking

When two people have a meaningful exchange, they both walk away feeling as though they have gained at least as much as they have contributed to the talk. It is not a one-sided conversation. This is not an investigation or a questioning. There won't be a string of uncomfortable pauses. It's like a gift exchange, where you give one and then get another in return. If you can perfect the art of conversation, not only will you spend less time feeling bored or worried with other people, but also the depth and quality of your professional and personal connections will increase.

Participate in idle chatter

Some people consider small talk to be taboo; yet, despite the fact that it is not the most satisfying form of discussion, it is both functional and essential. In the same way that a car needs to gradually accelerate to a specific speed rather than hitting 60 miles per hour all of a sudden, small chat is what leads the way to deeper conversation. Small talk sets the stage for more in-depth discussions.

If you're stumped for conversation starters, bring up the event you're attending, make a remark about the food or drink you'll be enjoying, or mention something interesting about the setting. Small talk ideas are easy to pull out. Because all of these events are universally experienced and can be related to by anyone, their application is universally applicable.

Be nice

This should go without saying, but make sure not to overlook it. Your level of friendliness can either make or shatter the other party's willingness to listen to what you have to say. Start the conversation with a wide grin and open body language, and keep the body language clear, your mind open, and your smile bright for as long as possible.

Make an effort to avoid crossing your arms, appearing distracted, or allowing your eyes to wander while speaking to someone. Keep eye contact whenever you can and make it clear that you are making an effort to listen to what the other person has to say by showing that you are engaged in the conversation.

Be Polite and Watch What You Say

In this context, I'm not suggesting that you should avoid using any profanity at all times. That is not at all relevant to the discussion. Streamlining the ideas that you communicate is the focus of this step.

When you "clean up" the ideas that you talk about, what you're really doing is getting rid of unnecessary details and filler material. When you are expressing yourself, making a point, making an argument, or telling a narrative, be sure that you just offer the most important elements. This is of utmost significance whenever you are speaking in front of a group, as you will only have a limited amount of time to explain yourself in such setting.

This exerts a significant impact on how others view you and the amount of influence you have over those around you. There is less noise as a result of the fact that you just communicate what is absolutely necessary to prove your point or tell your tale. People will have more time and energy to analyze and think about your ideas because they won't have to spend as much of that energy sorting through all of the superfluous information.

Polish Your Talk

People that are knowledgeable and successful tend to be able to say a great deal in a relatively short amount of time, as you may have noticed. They have perfected the art of dialogue and have found ways to streamline the way in which they express those thoughts. As soon as you begin doing this, you will be able to connect with a greater number of people in a shorter amount of time. You'll also find that the talks you have become richer in meaning and more fruitful.

Start with the assumption that you are unable to comprehend the other person

Always making an effort to grasp what the other person is saying is a fundamental component of effective conversation. You can demonstrate that you comprehend what they are saying by first questioning them, then restating what they said in your own words, and finally responding with something relevant to what they said.

On the other hand, in this case you have to perform the opposite action to move to higher levels. You make the assumption that you do not comprehend it. When you first meet someone, you are in a position where what they tell you is practically a mystery to you. Because of this, you are in an excellent position to use the art of conversation, which is one of the reasons why this is so beneficial to how you use it. You are intrigued, you have an open mind, and you are curious when you are in this position.

When you make the assumption that "you know what they're talking about," you prevent yourself from learning the most crucial information. You only acquire the surface level information and don't listen carefully enough to discover incredible things about other people. When you go into a situation with the mindset that you don't fully comprehend it, you drive your mind to unearth previously concealed treasures. These are fascinating specifics on the stories, ideas, or anything else that the other person is sharing with you.

They are more intriguing than anything else that is being said, but it is easy to lose out on them if you immediately assume that you grasp it, even if they are more interesting than anything else that is being said.

Take Care to Act in a Manner That Is Appropriate

When people get together with their friends, they want to be less formal and more intimate, and they sometimes even want to let their hair down. Even during professional networking gatherings, people make an effort to socialize with one another and be more authentic versions of themselves.

The takeaway here is that one should not be overly proper when interacting with people. That should give you the general concept. You've come to this place, though, because you want to learn about the art of conversation and graduate to more complex methods. The advanced advice for this situation is to be less formal, but to ensure that you are always formal, proper, and polite when necessary.

You demonstrate, on occasion, through the way that you speak, that you are capable of being formal and proper. You demonstrate that this aspect of you exists, and you are free to utilize it whenever you see fit. This understated action has the impact of demonstrating to your friends and friends of friends that they can rely on you in terms of social situations. They are aware that you are able to carry yourself in a manner that is proper in circumstances in which that is required.

A fundamental illustration of this would be the presence of an unknown person, one of their superiors, or a member of their own family. They are aware that you are able to behave in an acceptable manner and make them appear nice. Being personable, cheery, fun, and even goofy can be quite beneficial.

People want to be able to relax and have a good time with their friends, and that's exactly what they desire.

However, it is essential that you are able to act in the other manner, in a serious manner when the situation calls for it. Again, this is a very understated piece of advice. Even though you only use it occasionally, it has a lasting impact on people's perceptions of you and your business. Your buddies will begin to believe that they have complete control over where they can take you and who they can introduce you to.

Generate Enthusiasm in Conversation by Creating It

The reason I'm using that word in this context is to emphasize the idea that enthusiasm is something that must be purposefully created. It is not enough to be excited and hopeful when engaged in discussion when such feelings are already present in the air.

If you want to become an expert in the art of conversation, you need to demonstrate enthusiasm even when there is no obvious reason for you to feel that way. This is a crucial step in the process. And if you're wondering, "enthusiasm about what?" you're not alone.

The focus here should be on the interaction itself. You are hopeful and maybe a little bit excited about the possibility that the talk will go swimmingly and that it will be fascinating. Even at the beginning of a conversation with someone, you should convey additional positivity about what the two of you will discuss.

This has a significant impact on how others see you and what they think of you. You find yourself taking on the role of the person who is responsible for ensuring the success of the talks you have.

People who have conversation skills that are just average are not proactive and do not take leadership of the situation. They become enthusiastic whenever there is a reason to do so, regardless of the topic. They both feel and behave boring whenever there is even a remote possibility that the talk would be dull. Avoid acting in a rash manner. Be proactive, assume control of the situation, and bring passion and positivity to the conversation in order to make it more intriguing and exciting.

Share Some of the Things That Interest You

A person with mediocre conversation skills tends to keep to chatting about the same handful of topics whenever they meet someone new. This creates the appearance that the person has little options or capabilities. It would appear that they are restricted in terms of the topics that they can actually debate.

You do not want anything like this to occur to you at any point. You don't want people to worry what they could possibly discuss with you if you two were to ever meet up again, do you? You do not want them to have any uncertainties such as, "Well... they look nice, but I'm not sure whether we have much to talk about." It's common for this to happen, even to people who are truly intriguing and knowledgeable about a wide range of subjects.

The fact that they only discuss a few topics, however, gives the sense that they are restricted and perhaps even monotonous. To prevent this from happening, be sure to cover as many of the subjects that interest you as you possibly can. Every subject is intertwined with every other subject. You also need to seek out opportunities to present a comprehensive picture of the many facets of your life that particularly fascinate you.

It paints a comprehensive picture of who you are. And people have the misconception that there is a great deal they can discuss with you. You may, for instance, demonstrate some culture, intelligence, professionalism, physical exercise or sports, any intellectual interests you have as a side hobby, and describe some of the places you've traveled.

When you first meet someone, going over themes like that with them helps them rapidly comprehend the breadth and depth of the topics they can talk with you. Because of this, there is a greater chance that they will want to engage in many more interactions with you.

Work on Your Comedic Timing When You're Talking to People

Conversation requires the ability to defuse tense situations, lighten the mood when things are taking themselves too seriously, and connect with other people. Those that are skilled at conversational exchanges are able to do that. They may not necessarily make you laugh out loud, but they have a fundamental degree of competence and are capable of making you smile or crack a small smile.

This is significantly more crucial than most people realize. A strong sense of humor that you can draw on in difficult situations demonstrates that you have some life experience. It demonstrates that you are able to hold engaging and entertaining talks as well as that you have good social skills.

You'll find that you soon fall into the category of people who are able to have a good time with other people. You don't need to be hilarious to the extreme; you simply need to know the fundamentals. Timing and the element of surprise are crucial components of comedic delivery. You can learn about comedy by reading about it, but in my experience, the greatest approach to develop your comedic timing is to learn directly from your favorite comedians. You can read about humor if you want to.

Ask yourself, when you laugh at their jokes, what it is about your favorite comic that makes him or her so amusing. What was it about a certain remark or joke that made it so funny? Examine your assumptions about how the story will unfold and determine where those assumptions were wrong. Take note of the way the punch line is delivered.

It is not necessary that you think of yourself as a funny person in order to be able to achieve this. You don't even need to do that much analysis of the comedy that's being presented. The only thing you need to do is make it a habit to think about why the things that made you laugh are hilarious in the first place. Examine the phrase to see what it is in it that made you laugh, and try to understand why.

As time goes on, you will begin to develop some of that natural sense of humor and begin to employ it in conversation of your own accord.

Be at ease and just be yourself

It will be obvious to the other person if you are tense or if you are pretending to be someone you are not, which will doom the conversation to fail before it ever begins. It is true that if you are not actually calm, it is quite difficult to give the impression that you are. Relax and inhale deeply before continuing.

If you do not make an effort to calm down, you will find that you end up saying something that is either incomprehensible or irrelevant to what is being discussed (been there). Additionally, cultivate a kind grin; this will help you come off as approachable and nice to those around you. Important to keep in mind: if you give the impression of trying too hard to be someone or something that you are not, others will view you as a pretender or a want to be.

Walk up to someone and introduce yourself to them in order to kick off a discussion. To begin things off in a seamless manner is not only courteous but also essential. When the situation calls for it, you can give a handshake, and then proceed to smile and make eye contact with the other person. Simply extending a warm greeting puts the other person at ease and paves the way for them to share some information about themselves.

If your effort is not well received for whatever reason and you realize that the other person is being cool or standoffish, gracefully withdraw and go on. Do not interpret this as a sign of rejection; instead, think on the fact that the other person likely has good reasons for not returning your advances. It's possible that they are not feeling well, have had a rough day, or just aren't in the mood for conversation right now.

The Art of Conversation Is Something That Can Be Practiced!

When you go out to meet new people and observe some of those extremely skilled people having a conversation, it can be impressive to watch how they carry themselves. It would appear that everything they say is right on the money. They appear to be really skilled storytellers who are able to brilliantly communicate their arguments.

What you might not know is that the majority of the things that you overhear them say are things that they have spoken to other people in the past. After some practice, they are now able to deliver the lines with an almost flawless delivery.

In other words, kids receive the opportunity to practice telling those stories, using those language, and making those arguments. You might wish to consider following in their footsteps in this regard. Understanding that it is acceptable to be prepared and even rehearsed is the first step toward becoming a master of the art of conversation.

In order to be a better communicator, you need to practice telling your favorite tales and conveying your favorite thoughts and perspectives. Make the most of it. Even better, whenever you come across a new thought or narrative, immediately think ways in which you may share it to others and do this as soon as you can. Think about how you can phrase what you have to say so that others might take pleasure in it to the same degree that you do. Rehearse this in your head.

You need to come to terms with the fact that the way in which your ideas are organized in your brain is not the same as the way in which you should clearly convey those concepts. In a sense, you will need to translate the notion that you have in your mind into the idea that is articulated and communicated effectively.

For instance, the next time you listen to a podcast or watch a documentary and come away with a fantastic idea, try visualizing yourself sharing it with others. Even if you only do this for enjoyment, it will go a long way toward preparing you to convey your thoughts in a way that is very clear and concise.

Master The Art of Conversation

You must be more motivated than the average person if you want to become an excellent conversationalist. It's not enough to just be able to hold a conversation well. However, that is only the beginning of your capabilities.

You have the ability to attain a higher degree of competence as well as artistic expression, both of which will set you apart in a unique way. When people get to know you, they will automatically place you in a higher category.

They know quite immediately that you are one of those people who they want to have around. This is especially true if they are also skilled in the art of talking and possess excellent social skills.

People who are adept at social interaction find it simpler to trust and become friends with folks who are on the same social level as them. And it is not impossible for you to get that degree of conversational skill.

You need to educate yourself on it, put in the necessary amount of practice, and maintain appropriately lofty goals regarding it, all while avoiding taking it too seriously and being hard on yourself when you make errors.

11. Move Forward with the Best Version of Yourself

In order to be the best version of yourself, what do you need to do? Is it simply a matter of realizing your full potential? If you're like most people, you've pondered these issues as you look for a sense of self-worth, self-assurance, and purpose in your life. In order to reach your full potential and become the best version of yourself, you must start asking the tough questions when the answers you receive fall short of your expectations. This blog is dedicated to showing you how to make modest adjustments in your life right now to begin creating the best possible version of yourself!

Transform yourself into your ideal self

When reading self-help websites on gaining confidence, you'll often see this statement. But what does it really mean? Getting back to who you really are is the first step to being the finest version of yourself. Authentic self-discovery requires courage and determination, even if it appears simple.

To get to the core of who you are, you have to get rid of the false beliefs that cloud or distort your sense of yourself. (If you're worried about improving yourself, keep in mind that everyone is unique.) Using the success of another person's life as a yardstick is unfair because everyone's aspirations, goals, and abilities differ. Life also does not have a predetermined course or perfect outcome, as each person's path is unique and personal.)

Reconnecting with your true self

You must first discover the fundamentals of what makes you, you before you can begin creating the finest possible version of yourself. It is these foundations that establish who you are and where you situate yourself in the world: your values, interests, and passions. Sit in front of a mirror and ask yourself these questions:

What kinds of things do you like to do?

Is there anyone you love spending time with?

What kind of global influence do you hope to have?

What is the happiest moment in your life? When answering, don't be afraid to be genuine and honest.

Focus on how you're feeling while you ask yourself these questions, since every time that includes anxiety or anger, you're subconsciously telling yourself signals that keep the dialogue from moving forward. To better understand what's causing these feelings, let's take a closer look.

Are you worried that your search for identity will be a failure? Is there anything you're frightened of uncovering if you delve deep enough?

The truth is that no matter how simple or tempting it may be to feel inadequate, everyone of us is completely whole precisely as we are right now. The only way to overcome obstacles and become the best version of yourself is to get in touch with your core self. What is the secret to being the best version of yourself? Once you've determined who you want to be, you may devise a strategy for achieving that goal.

Begin by envisioning your ideal self, and then take tangible measures to get there. Here's how to get there.

Relinquish restricting assumptions Although you may be aware of who you are, what else are you capable of?

Most of us are stifled by self-defeating attitudes about our own limitations. In order to become the person, you truly are, you must learn to recognize and release any limiting beliefs you may have about your own abilities.

Use your strengths to your advantage

The more you focus on your strengths, the more capable you will become in those areas. When you reach a snag – and you will, we all do, it's normal – it's important to keep your eyes on your strengths. When you focus on what you do best, you're more likely to overcome any challenges that stand in your way.

Learn to see things from a growth perspective

There is no one who is simply made up of their best qualities. Personal concerns must be addressed if you want to become the best version of yourself possible. In order to be successful, you must have a growth mindset (A growth mindset means you appreciate taking on new challenges. Gaining new abilities or increasing your intelligence is something you're willing to work hard for. They don't think they have any flaws. There's always room for improvement, that's all. Instead than dwelling on their flaws, they look for ways to better – and then do something about it.

Throw aside any preconceived notions you may have had

What you think shapes your perspective on the world, but it's not always your own. You, like most of us, have developed a sense of self based on the expectations of others. In order to become a better version of yourself, you must learn to recognize the unconscious process of taking in other people's ideals. It is your vision for who you want to become, not anyone else's, so claim who you want to be!

Don't be afraid to let go of your former identity

The bar you set for yourself and everyone around you rises when you're on a mission to discover your ideal self. Feelings of insecurity and apprehension about the future will keep you from taking this step. Refrain from clinging to your old identity, which has been holding you back, and instead adopt a fresh, positive outlook on life.

Overcome your fears

When we are afraid, we lose our inherent courage and we are unable to focus on the here and now. The ability to overcome your fears is a necessity for personal growth. Make a list of the things you're frightened of while you're feeling worried. Once you've done that, come up with an alternate explanation that's both less terrifying and more likely to occur in reality. Even if your emotions don't shift immediately, your head will recognize the logic. You grow less susceptible to worry when the practice of fact-checking your fears becomes a habit.

Prioritize the outcomes

To become the finest version of yourself, you must look internally for wisdom, and you won't find it by reading a lot of books. Allow your ideal self to establish the objective for you. To begin started, choose something easy and attainable, such as organizing your home or reading more books. Getting out of your own head and establishing a foundation of self-belief begins with setting a specific, attainable goal.

Decide on attainable objectives

Setting simple, attainable goals will save you from becoming overwhelmed. Steps like exercising for 20 minutes each day or creating a daily schedule can help you lose 10 pounds and boost your productivity by 30%. To become the best version of yourself, you must take one step at a time toward your objective.

Create rituals that empower yourself

Successful athletes, entrepreneurs, and leaders all have one thing in common: they've improved upon their original selves to achieve their current levels of success. They all have one thing in common: they've cultivated habits that elevate them to greatness. To place yourself in an empowered frame of mind, you could try meditation or goal visualization. It's always a combination of healthy nutrition and regular exercise. Practicing thankfulness in your daily routines is often a part of this.

Be kind to yourself

Always keep in mind that being your best self is about you, not about what other people think of you. Stop comparing yourself to others and accept that everyone is on a unique journey. Don't berate yourself if things aren't going as planned. It is okay if you are at a crossroads; accept and move ahead from there. Take a break from social media or wallowing in self-pity over a recent loss and do something kind for yourself instead. Take a walk in the fresh air. Do something that you enjoy. Avoid self-defeating thoughts by speaking encouraging ones instead.

Effective self-management is essential

Developing excellent self-management skills is an important part of being the greatest version of yourself that you can be. Managing your time well frees you from stress, helps you become your ideal self, and frees you from the burdens of others' expectations on you. Keeping track of your success on a weekly, monthly, and yearly basis will keep you accountable and in control of your resources. Taking charge of your own schedule, whether it's for leisure activities or schoolwork, is essential for overall health and happiness.

Maintain an optimistic frame of mind!

Learning to be the best version of yourself comes with its share of challenges. Instead of giving up, focus on developing positive emotions like enthusiasm, intrigue, and adaptability in yourself and your work. Instead of seeing challenges as setbacks, consider them as steppingstones to greater success. By keeping a good attitude, you'll be able to think of inventive ideas that you wouldn't have otherwise.

12. Conclusion

Toxic thoughts can be said to be your worst enemy. That's right. It's not someone from the outside, it's the negative emotions that wreak havoc inside you and make you suffer. It all starts with accepting those emotions and then overcoming them and eventually, gaining complete control over them.

Anxiety, stress, panic, these are all mostly the byproducts of the toxic and negative thoughts which can be overcome with patience, diligence and a little bit of hard work.

I sincerely hope that this book was able to help you. May you come out as the best version of yourself after reading and implementing the techniques devised in this book!

13. References

1- K.S. LaBar & LeDoux, J.E. Emotional Learning Circuits in Animals and Humans. Handbook of Affective Sciences. Ed. R.J. Davidson, K. Scherer, & H.H. Goldsmith New York: Oxford University Press, 2003, pp. 52-65.

2- The Efficacy of Cognitive Behavioral Therapy: A Review of Meta analyses
https://www.ncbi.nlm.nih.gov/pmc/articles/PMC3584580/

3- Limbic System: Amygdala- Anthony Wright, Ph.D., Department of Neurobiology and Anatomy, McGovern Medical School- https://nba.uth.tmc.edu/neuroscience/m/s4/chapter06.html

4- Molecular Biology of the Cell. 4th edition. How Cells Obtain Energy from Food- https://www.ncbi.nlm.nih.gov/books/NBK26882/

5- Britannica, T. Editors of Encyclopaedia. "fight-or-flight response." Encyclopedia Britannica, August 12, 2019. https://www.britannica.com/science/fight-or-flight-response.

6- Emotional awareness- http://eqi.org/aware.htm#Definition

7- Evidence-Based Strategies to Manage Emotional Pain- https://psychcentral.com/blog/how-to-deal-with-emotional-pain

8- How to Identify and Express your Feelings- https://www.cognitivehealing.com/depression/learn-how-to-identify-and-express-your-feelings/

9- When Feeling Bad Can Be Good: Mixed Emotions Benefit Physical Health Across Adulthood- https://www.ncbi.nlm.nih.gov/pmc/articles/PMC376812 6/

10- The evolution of a fundamentally mindfulness-based treatment methodology: from DBT and ACT to MDT and beyond- https://psycnet.apa.org/fulltext/2014-38134-002.html

11- Effects of the dialectical behavioral therapy-mindfulness module on attention in patients with borderline personality disorder- https://psycnet.apa.org/record/2012-00309-001

12- Coping with Social Stress: Implications for Psychopathology in Young Adolescent Girls- https://www.ncbi.nlm.nih.gov/pmc/articles/PMC3117326/

13- Juth V., Dickerson S. (2013) Social Stress. In: Gellman M.D., Turner J.R. (eds) Encyclopedia of Behavioral Medicine. Springer, New York, NY. https://doi.org/10.1007/978-1-4419-1005-9_283

14- Common Sense Media. Tweens, teens, tech, and mental health. https://www.commonsensemedia.org/research/tweens-teens-tech-and-mental-health-coming-of-age-in-an-increasingly-digital-uncertain-and-unequal-world-2020

15- The Power of the Like in Adolescence: Effects of Peer Influence on Neural and Behavioral Responses to Social Media- https://journals.sagepub.com/doi/10.1177/0956797616645673

16- Smartphones, social media use and youth mental health- https://www.cmaj.ca/content/192/6/E136

17- Social media use and depression in adolescents: a scoping review- https://www.tandfonline.com/doi/abs/10.1080/09540261.2020.1720623?journalCode=iirp20

18- Using Many Social Media Platforms Linked With Depression, Anxiety Risk- https://psychnews.psychiatryonline.org/doi/10.1176/appi.pn.2017.1b16

19- Association of Digital Media Use With Subsequent Symptoms of Attention-Deficit/Hyperactivity Disorder Among Adolescents-

https://jamanetwork.com/journals/jama/fullarticle/268
-861

20- Sleepless in school? The social dimensions of young people's bedtime rest and routines- https://www.tandfonline.com/doi/abs/10.1080/1367626t .2016.1273522?journalCode=cjys20

21- How much sleep do I need? https://www.nichd.nih.gov/health/topics/sleep/conditio ninfo/how-much

22- The emotional responses of browsing Facebook: Happiness, envy, and the role of tie strength- https://www.sciencedirect.com/science/article/pii/S0747 563215003600X?via%3Dihub

23- Social Comparison Orientation and Cyberbullying Perpetration and Victimization: Roles of Envy on Social Networking Sites and Body Satisfaction- https://journals.sagepub.com/doi/10.1177/088626052110 23486

24- Panic disorder- https://medlineplus.gov/ency/article/000924.htm

25- Panic Attacks and Panic Disorder- https://www.helpguide.org/articles/anxiety/panic-attacks-and-panic-disorders.htm

26- Royal Australian and New Zealand College of Psychiatrists clinical practice guidelines for the treatment of panic disorder, social anxiety disorder and generalized anxiety disorder- https://journals.sagepub.com/doi/full/10.1177/00048674 18799453

27- Stress Management: Breathing Exercises for Relaxation - https://www.uofmhealth.org/health-library/uz2255

28- Stress Management: Doing Progressive Muscle Relaxation - https://www.uofmhealth.org/health-library/uz2225

29- Treating anxiety without medication - https://www.health.harvard.edu/mind-and-mood/treating-anxiety-without-medication

30- Mental Health Conditions – Panic Disorder - https://www.nhs.uk/mental-health/conditions/panic-disorder/

31- Substance Abuse Treatment for Persons With Co-Occurring Disorders. 9 Substance-Induced Disorders - https://www.ncbi.nlm.nih.gov/books/NBK64178/

32- Mechanism of Change in Cognitive-Behavioral Treatment of Panic Disorder: Evidence for the Fear of Fear Mediational Hypothesis - https://www.researchgate.net/publication/8408836_Mechanism_of_Change_in_Cognitive-Behavioral_Treatment_of_Panic_Disorder_Evidence_for_the_Fear_of_Fear_Mediational_Hypothesis

33- Hello, stranger? Pleasant conversations are preceded by concerns about starting on - https://psycnet.apa.org/record/2021-90811-001

34- Preferred Interpersonal Distances: A Global Comparison - https://bib.irb.hr/datoteka/873645.sorokowska_et_al_2017.pdf

35- Insufficiently complimentary?: Underestimating the positive impact of compliments creates a barrier to expressing them - https://psycnet.apa.org/buy/2021-92058-001

36- The thought gap after conversation: - https://psycnet.apa.org/buy/2021-92058-001

We always love to offer free books to our readers.

5 Simple Ways To End Anxiety and Panic Attacks

Get your free book by scanning the QR code or by sending an email to the address below.

Catherine.Worren@yahoo.com